Clockwork Classrooms

Solutions for smoother-running lessons

Carmel Bones

Together we unlock every learner's unique potential

At Hachette Learning (formerly Hodder Education), there's one thing we're certain about. No two students learn the same way. That's why our approach to teaching begins by recognising the needs of individuals first.

Our mission is to allow every learner to fulfil their unique potential by empowering those who teach them. From our expert teaching and learning resources to our digital educational tools that make learning easier and more accessible for all, we provide solutions designed to maximise the impact of learning for every teacher, parent and student.

Aligned to our parent company, Hachette Livre, founded in 1826, we pride ourselves on being a learning solutions provider with a global footprint.

www.hachettelearning.com

To order, please visit www.HachetteLearning.com or contact Customer Service at education@hachette.co.uk / +44 (0)1235 827827.

ISBN: 978 1 0360 0745 4

© Carmel Bones 2026

First published in 2026 by
Hachette Learning (a trading division of Hodder & Stoughton Limited),
An Hachette UK Company
Carmelite House
50 Victoria Embankment
London EC4Y 0DZ

www.HachetteLearning.com

The authorised representative in the EEA is Hachette Ireland, 8 Castlecourt Centre, Dublin 15, D15 XTP3, Ireland (email: info@hbgi.ie)

Impression number   10 9 8 7 6 5 4 3 2 1
Year   2030 2029 2028 2027 2026

Illustrations by DC Graphic Design Limited, Hextable, Kent.
Typeset in the UK.
Printed in the UK.

A catalogue record for this title is available from the British Library.

MIX
Paper | Supporting responsible forestry
FSC
www.fsc.org
FSC™ C104740

Reviews

Carmel's ideas are easy to implement and evidence-informed, stripping away unnecessary complexity and sharpening the small habits that make the biggest difference – helping classrooms run like clockwork.

Jamie Clark, author of Teaching One-Pagers *and dean of professional growth, Mercedes College, Perth, Australia*

Carmel uses her wealth of experience from the front and the back of the class to provide a how-to guide in creating an environment where students and teachers thrive. A must-have road map for the reflective teacher!

Ollie Claydon, headteacher of teaching and learning, Albion Park High School, New South Wales, Australia

Mixing anecdotes from her own career, research-based theories for long-term improvement and practical 'right now' strategies, Carmel provides a how-to manual that every teacher – regardless of their level of experience – should read.

Claire McInally, headteacher, St Thomas Aquinas High School, Glasgow, Scotland

A great read that provides teachers with lots of creative strategies to try in the classroom. It is written in such a positive way. I love the ideas. A highly useful toolkit.

Lorrayne Hughes OBE, CEO Cumbria Education Trust

Clockwork Classrooms is a user-friendly resource that has innovative strategies for practitioners at any stage of their career. The ideas can apply across any age group, subject area and education sector.

Caroline Gill, mathematics and physical education teacher, Clare High School, South Australia

This is a must-read book – it very clearly sets out many ways to help engage, inspire and enable children to enjoy learning and become successful. I like this book a lot!

Martin Murphy, CEO Arden Multi Academy Trust, Solihull, West Midlands

In a world that increasingly values individual achievement, this book offers a refreshing perspective on the power of collective strength in education. Carmel Bones beautifully weaves together research, personal anecdotes and actionable strategies, making a compelling case for building strong class camaraderie. Concepts such as 'Lesson of luxury' and 'Consensus – casseroling the conversation' are not just clever ideas; they're profound insights into nurturing a supportive and ambitious learning community. This book will make you rethink what's truly possible in your classroom.

James Nottingham, creator of The Learning Pit

Carmel Bones has skilfully distilled her unique blend of effervescent enthusiasm and practical pedagogy. The result is a handbook full of genius solutions to real challenges – instantly recognisable to all teachers. Carmel understands that effectively engaging learners is about harnessing their energy rather than exhausting our own. A very worthy addition to any professional reading library.

Ruth McKay, headteacher, Kirkwall Grammar School, Orkney

Based on sound theoretical research, this book is intensely practical throughout. For those educators who are searching for new methods of improving pupil performance and satisfaction, *Clockwork Classrooms* is a must-buy.

David Kemp, former head of St Aidan's County High School, Carlisle, and consultant in education management

Clockwork Classrooms is a powerful publication. It is jampacked with practical ideas and strategies to ignite learning in classrooms. For years I've wanted Carmel to be with me in school, sharing what she knows. Now, thanks to this book and her authorial tone, I feel like she is.

Dr Alex Fairlamb, educational consultant, Honorary Fellow of the Historical Association, co-author of The Scaffolding Effect *and co-editor of* What is History Teaching, Now?

Rooted in eminently achievable routines and habits that create powerful classroom culture, this book is an absolute page-turner for all teachers. Highly recommended.

Andy Buck, founder of Leadership Matters and BASIC Coaching

Every strategy presented has been researched, honed, tried and tested by an experienced, insightful author, whose warmth and personality shine through the book's pages.

Nathan Ashman, The Bishop Fraser Trust, Bolton, Lancashire

Student reflections

Carmel played a pivotal role in preparing for my application to Cambridge, going above and beyond. Her delight in hearing I had been successful meant a great deal. Clear and lofty expectations were set early in Carmel's classroom, and she equipped her students with the knowledge and skills needed to deliver these. She is an all-rounder with many qualities, but her ongoing support and belief in her students marks her down as someone special. My historical knowledge might have faded over time, but the lessons I learned from Carmel certainly have not.

Chris Humpleby, 33, jockeys' agent, Hawick

Mrs Bones instilled in me a love of history and inspired me to teach. She ran a training session at our school, and it was wonderful to be inspired by her again. I always hoped to be as good a teacher as her!

Rebecca Frank (nee Thwaites), 42, primary school teacher

The skills I developed in Mrs Bones' class have been invaluable in my professional life. Techniques employed to help us remember key events and dates whether through detailed notes or associative terms have stuck with me and proven to continue to aid my learning and retention in the workplace.

Doug Barber, 30, workshop manager and UK warranty handler

Carmel Bones is a force of nature in the classroom; her infectious passion has had an ever-lasting legacy on my own life and work. She develops a culture of ambition based on setting her students the healthy challenge of being the best possible version of themselves. Her unwavering belief, trust and support nurtured the historian in me and played a formative role in preparing me for my future academic endeavours.

Chris Law, 33, PhD candidate at Newcastle University
in collaboration with the Berlin Wall Foundation

I can honestly say I felt so confident and prepared to succeed when walking into the exam hall due to the support and coaching provided by Mrs Bones. Every lesson felt meaningful and was a building block in helping us achieve success. All the essays and feedback were targeted towards helping us to continually improve.

Declan Conley, 34, strategy and technical manager, BNFL

One of the things I reflect on the most is how inclusive Miss Fowler was. I'd arrived from another school and was in a class of peers who had already established relationships. Miss Fowler encouraged me to participate. I felt welcome; my confidence soared. I went on to be a first-generation university student.

Kelly Osgood, 46, head of teaching, learning and student experience, School of Environment, Education and Development, University of Manchester

Having Carmel's lessons in your timetable was like winning the school lottery. You'd look forward to them all week. The atmosphere was motivational, the pace appropriately challenging and the knowledge you came away with rewarding and enriching. Her innate passion for teaching is unquantifiable. You'd want to do well for yourself, but also for Carmel as your teacher.

Kelly Horley, 33, PR and external communications manager, and Luke Sawyers, 32, English teacher

Mrs Bones made me care about history. She brought stories alive: the highs and lows, the grim bits, the unbelievable parts. She knew how to reach children who were usually switched off; I had never seen that before. She was simply fantastic at teaching. She has remained genuinely interested in her pupils and is still so passionate about education, engagement and creativity.

Now, as a midlife single mother, there aren't many people who inspire me to believe I can do more than just scrape by. She made such an impact on me and still does.

Leah Irving, Carlisle, 42, meditation facilitator, holistic and sound therapist

Always positive and full energy, Mrs Bones meant business. Firm when she needed to be and soft at her core, she was a teacher I had respect for then and now. She demonstrated to us the belief that we could achieve whatever we put our minds to!

Gavin Chapman, 43, web/graphic designer

Carmel Bones made inclusive lessons fun and easy to understand. She always had time for every student. I could have gone to her with any question. She's a fount of knowledge and was a wonderful, patient teacher. Her lessons and approach to history are fondly remembered by me and my friends who had the pleasure of being taught and mentored by her through our teenage years.

Craig Muirhead, 39, hairdresser

Carmel has 33 years of experience working in schools. She has taught, observed or filmed over 20,000 lessons. Originally from Whitehaven in Cumbria, she was a history teacher and leader for 20 years before moving into a wider professional development role.

She was the host of the *Reteach History* podcast, and works with Osiris Educational, the British Library, the Premier League, BBC Bitesize, BBC Teach and ClickView. She has been a GCSE and A-level examiner and was part of the BBC Covid-19 Daily Bitesize Team. An honorary fellow of the Historical Association, she has also co-authored GCSE revision guides.

A regular speaker in schools and presenter at teacher and student conferences, Carmel's webinars form part of the CPD of hundreds of history departments. Listed in the EdTech 50 and shortlisted for various awards, she is honoured to be a judge to find the Inspiring History Teacher 2026.

Proud mother of two wonderful daughters, Carmel is a keen fell walker and runner, Carlisle Tri Club member and Carlisle Parkrun participant and volunteer.

Clockwork Classrooms is Carmel's first solo book. Inspired by a desire to help others and provide a shortcut to success, she was encouraged by all the students and colleagues she has had the good fortune to learn from and collaborate with.

You can connect with Carmel at www.carmelbones.co.uk.

Mam and Dad, Ellen and the late Frank Fowler, truly great parents.

David, my late husband and best friend.
We carry you with us in our hearts.

Niamh and Ciara, an awesome pair, I could not be prouder.
Keep smashing life – you are who I love!

Acknowledgements

This book is based on a lot of experiences. So many people have enthused and inspired me during my career and life. I want to acknowledge everyone I have ever shared or talked about being in a classroom with: initially during my own school days (the lifers!) as a classmate or student; professionally while undertaking my PGCE; then as a teacher, head of department, advanced skills teacher; and latterly when invited into schools to present, coach or collaborate. You all know who you are so give yourselves a firm handshake!

I floated the crazy idea of a book with my mam, Ellen. She said, 'Do it! You've been at it long enough and it's time to give something back.' She is a phenomenal person who, along with my late dad Frank, instilled the importance of education as a 'passport' from an early age. They fuelled my desire to take what goes on in the classroom pretty seriously and taught me the value of kindness, compassion and hard work. I hope this finished product makes them proud on Earth and in heaven.

The simply brilliant Kate Jones was a cheerleader from the start – so encouraging. Her foreword is unreal. Can't thank you enough, Kate.

Alex Sharratt, Anders Ingram, Alex Duffy and the team at John Catt took a chance on my idea and made things happen. I am so grateful you agreed to it! Thanks to Kate Daykin for kindly checking the legalities, and my editor Natasha Gladwell, an absolute gem – I couldn't have wished for anyone better.

Thanks go to all the schools, individuals and departments mentioned. To the generous reviewers for taking the time to read my unedited scribbling and sticking with it. I truly appreciate your kindness. Every teacher and school that has ever been part of my Osiris Teaching Intervention cohorts, you continue to shape my ideas. Every teacher who has ever attended a session in a school, at a conference or online, you have all pushed my creativity and made me think – thank you.

David Kemp, Natalie Packer, Jen and Mark Moody read and refined chapters without hesitation. Their input has made the book so much better. Georgie Lowry, Andrew Convery, Pete Murray and Phil Badham cast a creative eye over the cover, illustrative ideas and promo – thank you for your expertise.

The history community in various groups has been a constant source of support and inspiration. I would urge teachers to get involved in subject associations.

My incredible friends: Katie who has been with me for 50 years, Andrea, Anne A., Anne F., Caroline G., Caroline McB., Danny, Glenn, John, Karen, Katrina, Kay, Kerry, Lisa, Michelle, Sam and Suzanne – thanks for being there, listening and making me laugh. And thanks to 'the lads' – our best men Graeme, Jim, Paul and Steve with their daily wise words!

Away from the laptop, the entire Carlisle running community (trail, road, fell and Parkrun!) who are so supportive and ambitious for each other. Your constant invitations and cheerful camaraderie meant some kind of balance was maintained while I was writing.

And finally, my late husband David, who taught me so much. His legacy lives on in our beautiful, brave girls, Niamh and Ciara, who are my driving force.

Contents

Foreword

Clockwork Classrooms by Carmel Bones is a breath of fresh air in the field of books focusing on teaching and learning. The in-depth experience and expertise from the author shine through, with insights that can only come from someone who has spent significant time in classrooms. Undoubtedly, this is a very practical and helpful book for anyone working in a school environment. Each chapter offers authentic advice, practical techniques and meaningful takeaways for teachers at every stage of their career. There are sprinkles of anecdotes and heartwarming or humorous stories woven throughout. In an age where Generative AI is dominating headlines and discussions, this book highlights the role and power of the human teacher and connection in the classroom.

It's easy to overlook how crucial positive relationships and established routines are to effective teaching and learning, but Bones never does. For learning to get off to a great start, the teacher and students need to know and understand the boundaries and clear expectations within the classroom. Teaching and learning can sometimes be viewed through a separate lens to behaviour, with teachers encouraged to pick a lane – academic or pastoral – but effective teachers embrace both wholeheartedly. This book beautifully captures this explicit link between the behaviours, communication, interactions and responses and the progress made by learners.

Beyond establishing strong routines, Bones explores how to embed effective learning habits through embracing the findings from evidence, particularly the insights from cognitive science, and how teachers can apply that to their classroom context. Understanding how learning happens is crucial for the teacher and students. The book isn't bogged down in theory and jargon, but instead a refreshing combination of evidence and experience. Throughout the book, well-known sources in education are cited, alongside quotes from former students, and even lessons we can learn from football legend Jürgen Klopp!

I particularly enjoyed the chapter on 'Classroom connoisseurs', which captures the joy of refining our craft and striving for excellence without losing sight of the human heart of teaching, and it is also jam-packed with fabulous classroom strategies. Bones is unashamedly ambitious for students, while recognising the need for support, scaffolding and ongoing encouragement. Teachers will no doubt be grateful for the takeaway templates and tips, derived from an essential combination of evidence, experience and enthusiasm. I can see the potential for this book as not only helping individual classroom teachers and leaders, but also as a powerful prompt for group discussion and reflection, among departments or a whole school.

In a world where teachers are under increasing pressure and face numerous challenges, *Clockwork Classrooms* is a timely reminder as to why teaching truly is a privilege. I can imagine teachers scribbling down notes and looking forward to trying the numerous classroom techniques in their context. The author states her mission is to 'make lesson-life easier for dedicated teachers and learners'. I can confidently say to Carmel Bones, mission accomplished.

Kate Jones, senior associate for teaching and learning at
Evidence Based Education, teacher and author

How to use this book

There is no such thing as a 'clockwork' classroom, of course. We are intricate human beings dealing with intricate human beings, and all manner of things can propel us and derail us. Even though it is vital to keep this in mind, I have enjoyed seeing and sharing some atomic classroom habits; tiny, positive practical changes with remarkable recalibrating results (Clear, 2018).

This book is not about being robotic and regimented. I, my learners and colleagues are individuals, and we are far too expressive and free spirited for that. However, a chaotic classroom is not a good place for anybody to be either. It is soul destroying and damaging. Between the two extremes, the hope is to swing the pendulum in favour of calmness, creating an environment where the learning of new information or skills can be anticipated, expected and delivered.

The level of adjustment needed varies depending on the school, situation and starting point, and so this book is a pic 'n' mix of suggestions. Begin with whichever chapter takes your fancy. The list at the start of each chapter and the corresponding subheadings will help guide your decision. Have a look at the principles and strategies, and then choose what you'll try. Commit to action. Use the 'chapter walkthroughs' to work through the material (available at www.hachettelearning.com/john-catt-archive/john-catt-extras). The templates at the back of the book will help you to keep track and provide an opportunity for cognitive offloading. As time goes by, you can photocopy the templates and build up a running record of ideas and trials, charting your progress.

Enjoy the trial and improvement that experimenting with new ideas brings. I'd love to know how you get on. Do let me know what works, what you have learned, how your practice has changed and what challenges remain. Remember, 'be patient with yourself. Shouting at a flower won't make it bloom' (Mackesy, 2025).

Although new content is coming in England with a national curriculum from September 2028 and GCSEs from 2029, proven prime practice will underpin the changes.

Talk to and share ideas with your colleagues; a second set of eyes can help. They may also point out your strengths, which always need to be commended, celebrated and continued.

Good luck!

Carmel Bones, Carlisle, 25 February 2026

Introduction

How it all began...

Back in the spring of 1996, excitement was building in school for the European Football Championships to be held in England in June. Can we get off lessons? Can we wheel the telly in? How are we meant to focus? This was just the teachers! (I'm here all week...) It was a glorious time to be working with young people at St Aidan's County High School in the border city of Carlisle, with England and Scotland drawn in the same group!

During this time I was considering promotion to head of department, and one of my sixth formers (Brianna Parker) said, 'Don't bother, you'll spend the extra money on face cream and hair dye because then you'll have to do *everything*.' I thought, 'Wow! How insightful.' She was 17. I was 25. We were both so young. She was right, of course, and I am now buying face cream and hair dye. That's more to do with the passage of time, but this idea of 'who does all the work?' to keep things on track at a classroom, school and departmental level set off a train of thought.

I was teaching history with its substantive and disciplinary demands – they consumed my thoughts. I wrestled with how to learn more quickly, where best to place emphasis and the optimum running order for the scheme of learning. I was reading like crazy. My esteemed colleagues seemed to know everything about everything, and I was in awe of them. At weekends I was visiting local landmarks while trying to clue myself up on what was proximal to the learners so I could weave 'history around us' into my lessons. Content delivery was my focus. By recent standards, my thinking wasn't very diverse, inclusive or global. I was getting to grips with national curriculum levels, designing GCSE coursework and trying to keep ahead of my fabulous A-level students who were full of curiosity and questions.

Very gradually there was a change in my thinking. My focus shifted from thinking about myself and what I would say and do to deliver information. I started to think about how I could devolve more to learners. Each time the clock and bell signalled lesson changeover, there was one of me and roughly 30 of them. They gathered expectantly outside room 28, ready for their history lesson, mostly full of energy and enthusiasm, and I needed to work out how to harness this more.

I was so lucky to have the most experienced mentors to guide and encourage me. My patient and kind head of department Eleanor Paterson did it all. She'd appointed me as a newly qualified teacher (NQT) three years earlier (the equivalent of an ECT – early career teacher – today). On the interview panel she was the benevolent member smiling all the time. I thought I was in. I later discovered she had been smiling at everyone who faced her across that scary desk! Alongside Eleanor was the headteacher, David Kemp. Earlier on the interview day, this tall, imposing gown-clad figure almost floated over to the candidates. He was straight from assembly exuding gravitas. He approached us and revealed he was a member of the history department, which in his words was 'the *best* department in the school' so this appointment was of 'particular importance' to him.

David was simply brilliant, flanked by two deputies – the 'A team', as he called them – both of whom led the school following his retirement. Firstly, the beloved and much-missed Jean Wirth and secondly, the indefatigable Martin Murphy. My professional mentor, Jean was ahead of her time in so many ways; a truly wonderful person. She guided us all, including Martin. Martin was the charismatic deputy who carried the baton to further develop and expand the school, maintaining its place as the best in the city – as far as we were all concerned at least! School life was hectic. We were always up against the clock and we crammed so much in. According to Ofsted, we were 'a school full of life'.

Like most teachers globally we were largely ruled by the bell, yet we met daily in a communal staffroom for 20 minutes at breaktime, swapping student stories and planting the seeds of CPD ideas. This natural way of engaging by uniting and reflecting mirrored desirable features of the April 2024 EEF (Education Endowment Foundation) guidance on implementation of meaningful and long-lasting changes.[1] Turns out, over the coffee, biscuits and breakfast butties, we were cutting edge!

Daily conversations with others from across the school helped me develop a holistic view of education and a deepening respect for the distinctive nature of the different disciplines and how talented and brilliant my colleagues were. We were an eclectic mix, hardly any shiny shoes or cuff links – more elbow patches and lab coats – but we were, in the main, passionate enthusiasts. I realised we were all ambitious for our learners,

---

1 'A school's guide to implementation', EEF (educationendowmentfoundation.org.uk).

and as a collective we tried to forge links, reinforce messages and devise meaningful cross-curricular enquiries. When I talk to early former learners now, many of whom are in their mid- to late forties, they talk so fondly about their time at school. We reminisce and they tell me how much they knew the teachers cared. I felt privileged and lucky to be working with subject specialists and young people from whom I could learn so much, and over 30 years later, I still do.

For an hour a week Jean stopped the clock for the NQTs. We had tea and cake in her office, and she asked us to share our triumphs. Her approach was a psychologically safe one before this was even a well-known concept! 'Tell me what great things have been happening in your classroom' was always her opening gambit. She asked us what we were struggling with and gave practical suggestions for improvement. 'Failure' was a natural part of learning, and we felt comfortable with being candid. We were openly new and inexperienced 'don't knowers', keen to trial and improve. Sam Crome (2023) explores these ideas and the work of Dr Amy Edmondson in his book *The Power of Teams*. Jean was encouraging our collegiality and camaraderie. I sensed she viewed the staff like the learners – a team with different strengths and starting points. I started to see the parallels and applicability to the classroom. Happy days – I couldn't have had a better start to my teaching career.

The start of clockwork classrooms

In a bold continuing professional development (CPD) move, David Kemp took the whole staff to the state-of-the-art Nissan car factory in Sunderland. Some teachers were chuntering (love that word) on the coach about how ridiculous it all was that we were being dragged across the country after school to see an irrelevant car plant. How wrong they were! To see the marginal gains made along the assembly line and how everyone was constantly looking to make things quicker and slicker was a revelation. It was a team effort, with collective efficacy and shared goals and outcomes. All employees were involved in refining business processes to raise quality standards, cut costs and reduce wasted time. This continuous improvement known as *kaizen* – a Japanese business philosophy – became the watchword on the corridors at St Aidan's. While teaching and learning is clearly not about cars on an assembly line or tins of beans on a conveyor belt, it is evident that educational research in the 21st century increasingly aims to consider and even control variables. Devoting time to reflecting and refining became part of the 'platinum model' of school improvement, the favourite phrase of my third headteacher, the maverick Martin Murphy.

This Nissan visit inspired me to think further about mass production, the tightly managed operation and 'clockwork' nature of factory working and how, if at all, I might apply *any* of this to the role of head of department in a school. I didn't follow Brianna's advice; I applied for and was delighted to be appointed to head of department while Eleanor was rightly promoted to deputy head. Time management became an even bigger issue. Now I wasn't just running my own classroom (with Eleanor on speed dial), but I was also mentally managing what was going on in 12 people's rooms, ensuring consistency, quality lessons and living up to the established high standards and expectations.

Soon after, I was lucky enough to hear Dylan Wiliam speak. It was a bright Monday morning, and we had excitedly (some of us at least!) gone as a staff to a local hotel along with colleagues from neighbouring schools. Packed together in the unfamiliar grand surroundings, I tried to keep up with the lecture and was pulled up short when Wiliam said, **'The receiver of the feedback should work harder than the person who gave it – is that true in your classroom?'** By this point I was looking at my shoes. I had spent Sunday marking Year 12 essays with detailed written feedback knowing full well the receivers would say to each other, 'What did you get?' Dead stop. I was thereafter on a mission to devolve, subtract and simplify wherever possible.

I was influenced in this regard by my late mathematician husband David Bones. We met as PGCE students. He was an incredible teacher always looking for efficiencies and the shortest point between A and B. 'Expedite the process' was his mantra. His results were off the scale. He too was ahead of his time. As early as 1993 he used to say, 'Marking by teachers is overrated and will become a thing of the past.' He was all about being responsive – giving feedback in the moment. The debate is alive today outlined brilliantly by Kate Jones (2024) in chapter one of her book *Feedback: Strategies to Support Teacher Workload and Improve Pupil Progress*.

David's reference from his first headteacher, Tony Webster, at Queen Elizabeth High School, Hexham read, 'To whom it may concern, employ this man.' That was it! David was so modest he'd never, ever tell anyone this, but I thought it was brilliant. Webster's words also got me thinking, no time had been wasted here – clockwork.

After running my own classroom, then the department, then becoming an advanced skills teacher (AST) within the county, I have now moved into a wider roving professional development and learning role. Enlisted by senior teams I have been very fortunate to spend time in schools videoing thousands of lessons across the curriculum, and I have seen incredible teachers in action. All are ultimately trying to do the same thing – be ambitious for their learners, provide them with new information and widen their horizons. They care, support, nurture and enthuse – all the amazing things teachers do. My travels between schools involve training, coaching, teacher self-reflection, celebrating successes, building confidence, and identifying and implementing ways of being more impactful.

The importance of 'clocking on'

However, it really saddens me now to read of some learners not enjoying or attending school (Gov.uk, 2024). The number of severely absent children was 150% higher in 2023 than before the Covid-19 pandemic, with one in 50 children missing at least half of lessons (Adams, 2024). This represented 2.14% of learners and stubbornly increased to 2.26% in autumn 2024/ spring 2025. Persistent learner absence in England (the proportion of pupils missing 10% or more of their classes), which was as high as 24.2% in autumn 2022–23, fell to 19.4% 2023–24 (TES, 2025). The latest data shows a pleasing continuing decrease to 17.63% for autumn and spring terms 2024–25. I know times have irrevocably changed. There are many issues at play and wide regional differences, and the greatest increase is among those who are most vulnerable. Sadly, significant barriers remain for some children and reasons often lie outside the school gates.

Unsurprisingly, there continues to be a positive correlation between increased attendance and attainment. The impact is significant. Missing 10 days of Year 11 (final year of compulsory schooling in England) can reduce the likelihood of a grade 5 in English and maths by around 50% (DfE, 2025). We are learning all the time, but my classroom and school experiences have shown me what works to enable learners and teachers to thrive.

Teacher recruitment and retention figures are gloomy too.[2] The teacher workforce in England grew by just 259 in the year to November 2023. One in 10 teachers in England leaves within the first year and 32.5%

---

2   See: https://epi.org.uk/publications-and-research/six-charts-that-explain-the-state-of-the-teaching-workforce-in-england/

leave within three years. Teacher-to-learner ratios in secondary schools in England are at their highest on record – a shocking 16.8 learners to one teacher (Booth, 2024a). Harnessing the agency of these young people is vital to prevent teachers becoming overwhelmed and learners becoming passive passengers due to understandable classroom wait times.

Thankfully attendance is currently a part of government focus. They have set a sector target of 94%, which would equate to children attending 20 million more days of school each year from 2028 to 2029 (DfE, 2026).

How Clockwork Classrooms can help

This book is based on what I have seen while closely observing lessons over three decades. Knowing 'what to look for when you're looking' is notoriously difficult. We know what we like, and learning is invisible, so we can tend to focus on observable proxies for learning (Coe, 2024). The use of video to capture the lesson experience has been very powerful – the most common teacher reflection has unsurprisingly been that it's like holding up a mirror! The following chapters are born out of the encouragement of colleagues I have worked alongside who have implied that documenting these approaches, ideas and reminders would be useful, especially in an interactive way. I will be offering suggestions to assist with the smoother running of lessons rooted in classroom practice.

My mission is to make lesson-life easier for dedicated teachers and learners. You will invariably find your own way forwards depending on your learners, set-up and capabilities – one size rarely fits all. I learned this early on as a Saturday sales assistant on the pic 'n' mix counter in Whitehaven Woolworths back in the 1980s! Despite having an assortment of about 50 sweetie options, I was guaranteed to hear a disgruntled cry of 'Have you no coffee creams, lass?' Sometimes my lunchtime cover slot on records was a welcome relief! The hope is that you will pic and mix ideas that suit your context and style, and maybe you'll put your own spin on them. Take a risk, be adventurous and sample some new flavours!

I have not worked with big datasets; the reflections are taken from working at a micro level. To quote Peter Blatchford (Amass, 2024), I'm aiming to 'get to grips with what I think is the most important thing, which is the immediate classroom context and interactions and relationships within the classroom: we might say the more proximal as opposed to distal factors'. What I have noticed initially is that teachers often speak generally: 'They're a good class.' 'They're a bad year group.' 'The girls are terrible.'

While we should avoid sweeping generalisations, it's an understandable pitfall, but we should try to remain discerning, step back and look. It's not easy, but it's incumbent upon us to take a nuanced approach. There is nothing worse than a teacher seeing that one person doesn't understand and stopping the whole class, or alternatively, when one person is disruptive or misses a homework and everyone is tarred with same brush. That can build resentment, and a huge part of a teacher's role is to have whole-class awareness and realise the differences between individuals. Figuratively speaking, try to avoid letting the tail wag the dog.

Teachers and learners are unique – this book respects that. A new term has recently been coined to reshape how the sector approaches professional development – 'didagogy'. It describes the teaching of teachers as distinct from the teaching of children. 'If pedagogy shapes the classroom, didagogy shapes the profession' (Gibbs and Bean, 2025). It considers not only the practices and techniques being conveyed, but also the conditions linked to the school or trust culture and context, as well as the identity, motivations, expertise and needs of the individual teacher. This book aims to acknowledge all three elements. The hope is that you can autonomously integrate ideas that meet your particular needs and connect them to your context to improve practice. There are templates at the end of the book that may be of use to keep track of what works when, why and how, and 'chapter walkthroughs' are available at www.hachettelearning.com/john-catt-archive/john-catt-extras.

This book is about rigour, expectations, habits and consistency, and it is designed to make your time in the classroom easier and more enjoyable. I truly hope you are energised to find some beneficial takeaways within its pages.

Chapter 1 map

High expectations

1	Keep sourcing the intel – teacher detective
2	Register routine
3	Register race
4	Need to know – closing the gap
5	Home and away seating
6	A second set of eyes
7	Classrooms as an 'elite context' – stadium seating
8	Gather and go
9	Tune in: the importance of listening and quiet time
10	Word up: etymology and morphology
11	Running records
12	MEOW

Chapter 1:
High expectations

A rising tide lifts all boats[3]

Welcoming a new class is an utter privilege and great responsibility. Impressionable young people are there to learn in the widest sense of the word. Learn about your subject, learn about themselves, learn about each other. These are formative years. Character is being shaped, and teachers should realise the impact they have. It is important that learners know you are ambitious for them and care about their learning from the outset. This sets the tone and leads to smooth running lessons. You are a role model. You need to establish and maintain high expectations in all areas, for a good beginning makes a good ending. The learners need to be 'bothered' enough to get involved: 'all learning is about cultivating desire' (Christine Counsell at the Historical Association conference in 2016). The early period of taking on a new class is like preparing the ground. It is the foundation of all that follows. It can be hard to claw things back if standards are not initially clearly high. To quote the great Bill Rogers, 'You establish what you establish' (Sherrington, 2018).

Remember the anticipation you felt as a young person in school when you first received your timetable? 'Who have we got for English?' It is hopefully exciting, it's significant and it can of course stir up a range of emotions in young people. As teachers we hope to smooth the passage as best we can. There is a sense of expectancy, not to mention the obligatory colour coding and shading in of matching lessons on the printout that might follow, by some learners at least!

Your overall aim is to show that you mean business. By that I mean there must be clear purpose, so inclusion and early challenge are important.

---

3   A phrase popularised by John F. Kennedy.

Design initial tasks that require participation, definite contributions and thinking. Make sure the participation ratio is as high as it can be. In order to motivate, most classes or individuals require the taste of success over struggle. Others prefer the challenge of wrestling with material. You will learn more about starting and staging points as you work with the group. 'To get a habit to stick, you need to feel immediately successful – even if it's in a small way' (Clear, 2018).

This opening chapter provides some tried-and-tested guidance on how to transmit a culture of high expectations, not only on your part, but also by learners of themselves and each other. It's complex and variables are interconnected – no one is suggesting otherwise. I have done the labour-intensive work of scrutinising thousands of lessons in the hope of gathering some takeaways that you might like to try.

The ideas are largely sequential, but can be used in tandem too. There is overlap, and often the answer is frustratingly 'it depends', but what is for sure is these young people are depending on you to help them reach their potential, so let's make a start!

1. Keep sourcing the intel – teacher detective

Finding out about your learners to build relational trust is key to a smooth passage over the time you are together, no matter how long that is. It could be that these learners are solely your class for 12 months or just a term, or you share them, or you could encounter the group en masse or as individuals for five to seven years. Whatever the permutation or duration, it helps to immediately develop win–win interactions by finding out what makes learners tick. Use whatever background information you are supplied with to inform you, but be sure to be open-minded and make your own mind up too.

I started at a new school with a new A-level class, a tough gig when you have no previous experience with the school or the learners. I quickly realised I needed a fast-track way to get to know this large class of 16–17-year-olds, so I chanced my arm and just asked them. I gave the learners a blank sheet of paper and asked for their history, a bio – a pen portrait, if you like. No word limit (I figured this might tell me something about them too) and the learners all willingly told me as much as they wanted to. One learner wrote along the lines of 'I have never been asked about myself before.

Thank you for finding out what I might like or what might help me.' I was stunned. This was a paper-and-pen exercise, but it worked.

There are so many online forms that can be used now: Wayground (formerly Quizizz), Mentimeter, Socrative, OneNote to name but a few. I have seen these used brilliantly, particularly at Portobello High School in Edinburgh by Anna Kirkwood in English and David McCreath in geography. Some learners tend to be more honest and open using this digital way of working. How you go about gathering information might well differ depending on your context.

Throughout this book, my aim is to respect your unicity – a highly prized teacher characteristic. The main message is to be a teacher detective, open to new information, finding out and then using this to optimise outcomes for your learners by appealing to them, making links and forging reciprocal, unconditional positive regard.

2. Register routine

The register – a basic. It's a legal requirement in some places. We all must do it. Even remembering to do it can be a challenge.

I was always being chased up by the school office because I'd be so focused on lesson content delivery, I'd forget this vital piece of admin. I needed a routine. But first there is the task of mastering the learners' names, and quickly. You must have a handle on who is and isn't there during the lesson.

Making visible how you initially intend to commit the names to memory is a great levelling opportunity; a chance for you to immediately reveal your own hand as a struggling learner too.

You have before you: a new class, new people to get to know, new names, new discoveries to make. You don't know what they can and can't yet do. Cognitive overload is apparent, with potentially overwhelming information coming at you from all angles, which is hard to process. Cognitive offloading techniques are external tools or methods to lessen the mental effort needed for tasks (more about cognitive offloading in section six of chapter six). We are all different and a classroom plan or diagram might be a handy organiser for you to refer to if needed.

The first job is to model how you'll remember the names. Celebrate this learning of new information. Set yourself that challenge and make it clear. Show that you are a learner and your desire (and associated struggle) to commit this information to memory is seen through deliberate practice and repetition – the class will urge you on!

I devised a **register ritual that becomes a routine.** I have done this for years and it has worked a treat. So, while you are making a performance out of it, you are making learning visible and showcasing a *desirable difficulty*. This is a phrase first coined by Robert Bjork in 1994 as I came to the end of my first year of teaching. In short, the premise is that the long-term benefits of mastering something tricky are greater compared to an easier task.

In this case you're facing the class, looking them in the eye and retrieving the names from memory. Now you are (perhaps unwittingly, I didn't realise this until I thought about it and broke it down) demonstrating the five principles of learning from the cognitive science model of memory (Pearce and Moore, 2024).

The five principles of learning from the cognitive science model of memory (as applied to taking the register!)

1. **You need to pay attention and think hard, making memorable associations.** For instance: Barry = brown hair, Sean = smiley, Rebecca = ribbon. Whatever might make the name memorable for you. You might use the order of seats: Wayne, Donna, Jade, Sharon, Stuart would become WDJSS. Rehearsing this during lessons, encouraging questions and verbalising your metacognitive thinking helps learners to develop theirs. 'Modelling by the teacher is a cornerstone of effective teaching' (EEF, 2025).

2. **Working memory is limited when we learn something new.** I've only ever been able to remember about six to eight names at a time, which is in line with Miller's Law. George Miller's often cited 1956 paper explains that our working memory can generally hold seven pieces of information, plus or minus two. So by chunking the information (the order of seats technique mentioned before), we can demonstrate to our learners how to more efficiently process and remember more information. This 'choke point' (Harvard, 2025) is shared and a solution to overcome it explained.

3. **What we already know determines what we learn and how quickly.** Prior knowledge is important here. You may have taught siblings or there may not be anything you can draw upon. Make this

point to the learners too. It's easier because you already have a hook into the new information, a network of knowledge to draw upon. This is schema theory. David Ausubel in 1968 knew this: 'the most important single factor influencing learning is what the learner already knows' (quoted in McLeod, 2024). Woah! This stopped me in my tracks. It's an important sentence; I'm tempted to write it twice.

4. **Fluency arises through practice over time.** This investment of time is worth it. Challenge yourself. Pick a timeframe appropriate for your context and set a target. For example: 'In three weeks' time, I'll be able to take this register in three minutes.' Deliberately and ceremoniously do it lesson in, lesson out, making mistakes as you go with judicious use of the timer.

5. **There is a paradoxical relationship between learning and forgetting. To remember stuff, we must forget it!** The process of learning is counterintuitive and the spaced nature of your lessons forces a time lapse. Spacing has been shown in numerous studies to promote long-term retention. Taking the register is retrieval practice in action. Of course, you have no real control over how often you see the group, and when it comes to learning and curriculum design, the spacing needs to be planned, but you can make the point in a tangible way and learners will see and feel the benefit of your efforts. See Doug Lemov's annotated version of the Ebbinghaus curve here for an excellent explanation of the relationship between learning and forgetting.

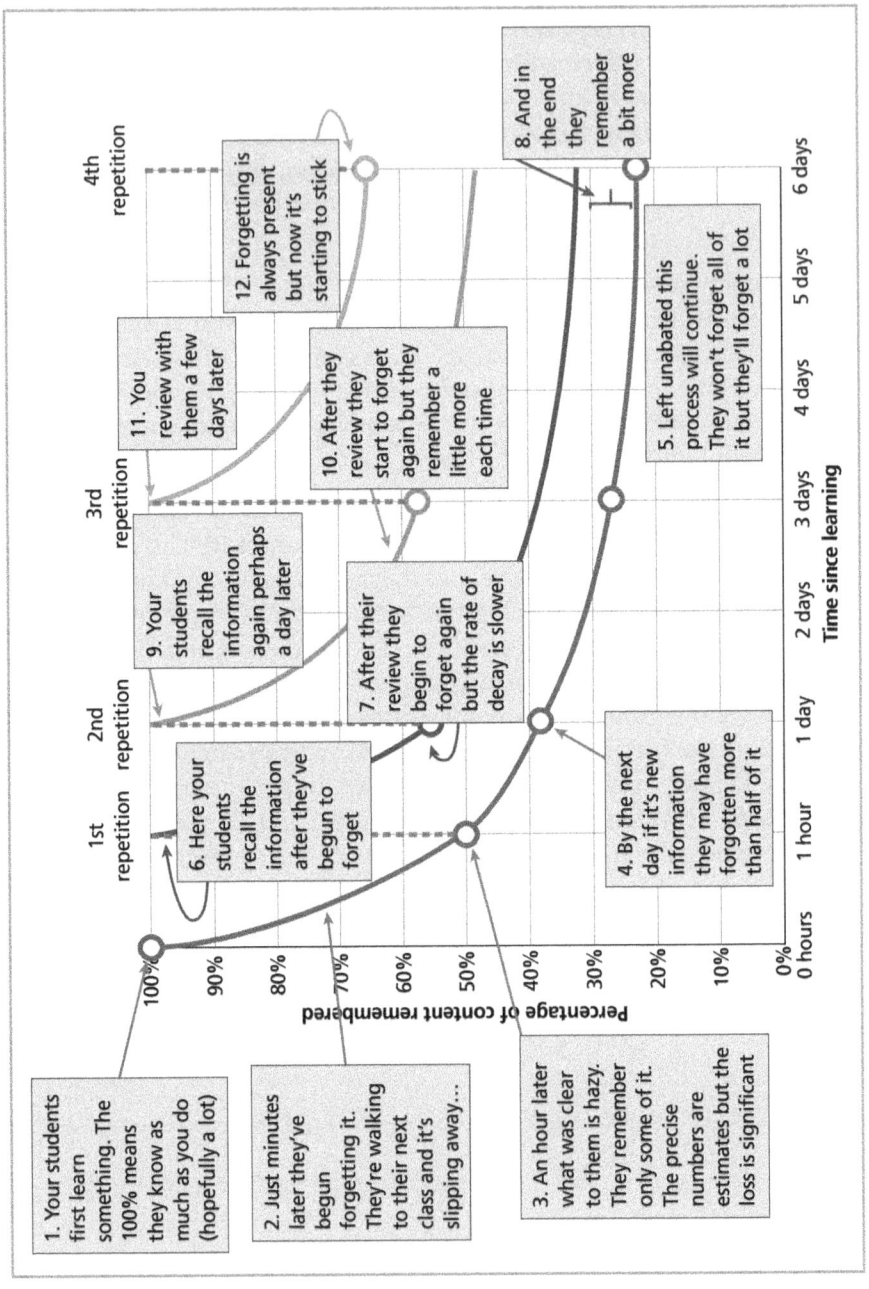

Often learners have come from the same feeder schools and might know each other. They will certainly know each other more than you do, initially at least. You might have encountered some learners at a transition or introductory event, but essentially you are an absolute novice who will become an expert before their very eyes. It's like magic – don't miss this opportunity! Harness the overlap between the informal and formal aspects of learners working together (as said by Peter Blatchford in Amass, 2024). The earlier learners appreciate that you are striving for success and ambitious for them, the better. You are defining what will constitute excellence and setting high expectations of yourself and for your learners. The register is memorable because it is all about them, so they are all invested and willing you on. Your increasing success will be a blueprint for motivation.

When you first start, demonstrate how low your starting point is: you genuinely don't have a clue. 'Are you Sydney?' 'Are you Lee?' The class will be laughing with you.

Laughter and joy can be practical tools that not only aid memory but also serve to integrate and include learners within the classroom. The historian Mary Beard has written that in Ancient Rome there were 'designated "laughter makers" in the imperial palace and other elite contexts' (Beard, 2014). In modern day elite sport, successful 'coaches such as Gareth Southgate and Sarina Wiegman create environments characterised by fun and flair, support and compassion [in] preparing for world-class performance' (Bishop, 2024). Why we laugh is as mysterious now as ever it was, but if it was good enough for the Ancients, then maybe we too can learn to enjoy the power of laughter in our classrooms. I very much like the idea of the classroom being an 'elite context' too!

By sharing this register routine experience and working collaboratively, you and your learners are in fact becoming what Bruce Daisley calls in his book *Fortitude* **synced, aligned and connected**. Singing or drumming similarly establish a sense of community and feeling of 'being in sync' with those around you (Daisley, 2023). This moving from modelling to autonomy along the 'I do, we do, you do' continuum early on can help make individual class members feel part of something bigger. It can break down feelings of isolation and lead to connection. It is a communal act that everyone must be part of. Lifts in endorphin levels come when individuals experience a pleasurable and reassuring sense of togetherness, making individuals feel part of something shared and therefore less anxious or isolated. The same is true of marching, eating together, or attending a match, festival, religious gathering or concert. It also probably explains the weekly mass appeal of Parkrun in recent years, with 11 million people globally signed up. Synchrony enthuses and motivates, making us feel positive and engaged, connected at a deeper, more meaningful level. It adds expectancy and certainty to those early lessons, possibly helping to remove any anxiety and make learners feel an early sense of camaraderie and belonging. The world is much worse without it, as many people sadly experienced during the Covid-19 pandemic.

Because you have set yourself a high challenge from first meeting the class by demonstrating the register routine as a *desirable difficulty*, this ritual will hopefully enable you to model perseverance. You have not shied away from doing something tough. James Nottingham takes this further with a 'Learning Pit' (Nottingham, 2023) idea, using a metaphor of being stuck in the pit and strategically working a way out – a collaborative endeavour – before reaching the 'Eureka, I've got it!' mastery moment. Your learners will see you visibly on this learning journey as in time you will fluently recall their names without reference to any list.

In the long term, the fact that you are proficient, able to scan, recognise, remember and keep ongoing tabs on learners is very helpful for teacher credibility and learner accountability. It allows you to be one step ahead and learners know you're on it. Your learners will notice you are with it, which is helpful for cementing authority.

Demonstrating your struggle and success might propel learners to close their own knowledge gaps and face up to what they can or can't do. Without getting too heavy, learners now have a proximal daily anchoring point reminder: 'Remember me trying to learn your names? Now you, dig deep.'

3. Register race

Building on register routines, once you have moved from novice to expert in terms of learners' names, you can transfer the expectancy and excitement by playing 'register race' – a genius idea courtesy of the Sunderland-based expert history teacher Lesley Ann McDermott. In this instance when you call the register, rather than responding with their name, learners reply using a word, concept or idea linked to a key topic you have launched as the focus.

So, let's say the topic is chemical elements. When you say each learner's name, they must say the name of a chemical element. Now, clearly there needs to be more responses than there are learners. As with most things it works best if you tee the learners up and perhaps say, 'Tomorrow we will be playing register wars,' so the class are ready in advance. Also, if you have the holding slide 'Register race – chemical elements' as learners arrive in the classroom, they can be jotting words in the back of their books ready for the register to begin. This can easily be applied to any subject area – have a think. Learners should not repeat what another classmate has said (so peer listening is encouraged). Clearly you will need to judiciously mix up the register order using what you know about your learners to optimise outcomes, otherwise it's a bit unfair on the person who has a surname beginning with Z!

There are a couple of variations here. You can make it a race and set a timer so the class try to get faster or at least have it done in, say, two minutes. Or, depending on what you'd like as an outcome, perhaps have a keyword in mind, listen to the responses more slowly, responding accordingly, and reveal who said your keyword and why you had chosen that word at the end. It might be that word had previously been misunderstood, misused or misspelled, or it needs further emphasis for whatever reason. Feel free to call this 'register wars' as an alternative to add some variation to this theme of recall, where the goal is not to be the fastest, but to give the best response. The power of synchrony is here again: 'when we feel part of a group and in sync with it, we experience a protective glow. Self and other overlap and our sense of identity flourishes accordingly. Anything that disconnects us from the group has an invisible but potent adverse effect on our well-being and, by extension, on our fortitude' (Daisley, 2023). So it is important to look for opportunities to engender these feelings among young people, so they feel as though they belong and with this, increasingly develop a sense of pride.

Clearly, to play the game **the learners must be provided with the tools of the trade**; the specialist disciplinary words they need to access your subject. Very early on in the teaching I provide glossaries or word lists, so learners are equipped. This means they have choices and options; they have the kit so they can increasingly speak like a scientist, write like a historian or read like a geographer. An important and underrated classroom skill in my view is listening to peers. Christine Counsell (2024), a commissioner on the Oracy Education Commission (chaired by Geoff Barton), wrote at its launch: 'A curriculum should leave learners bursting to talk – having something to say, a burning desire to communicate it, confident oral expression, wide vocabulary, skill in argument and a will to listen.' The importance of oracy has been further strengthened in the 'Curriculum and assessment review report' (Francis, 2025).

4. Need to know – closing the gap

'Our brains were designed for having ideas, not holding them' (Caviglioli and Goodwin, 2021), so there might be stumbling blocks when taking the register too, such as learner names you simply find harder to commit to memory than others. Emphasise and face up to these gaps in your knowledge and show the class how you need to close them. **In so doing, you are demonstrating self-scaffolding techniques.** This is something the learners can hopefully transfer to their own learning. Perhaps encourage them to have a 'need to know' page wherever they keep their notes. Here they can draw symbols, emojis, mnemonics, whatever it takes to help them remember or make tricky bits of information sticky. This way, they will keep a running record of what they need to know. We all have different ways. Share with the whole class how you remember information using rhymes, analogies and associations to go beyond remembering and teach for understanding (Newton, 2000). We are all 'don't knowers' at first, so make sure you are humble enough to acknowledge this.

Most importantly, make closing those gaps part of the classroom routine – an atomic habit. This cannot be emphasised enough. It is something I have noticed that learners rarely do automatically. Somehow it has been overlooked or neglected, and teachers try in vain, often retrospectively, to reinforce the importance of it. Sometimes the learners are already in the habit of *not* doing it. Explicitly teaching learners how to effectively manage their learning independently can be very impactful. The younger the age at which learners understand the need to close the gap, the better. Gap closing is where it's at! This is such a worthwhile goal and should ideally be part of learners' armoury of self-regulation strategies, particularly helpful when it comes to formal external exams. There are all kinds of graphic organisers that learners can use to map their knowledge and make connections, which can help them marshal their knowledge and corral it when needed (Caviglioli and Goodwin, 2021).

5. Home and away seating

Seating plans can be a hot teaching topic. If you're intending to implement 'register routine' to make life easier, it is best to keep learners in their original seats (however you initially decided them), in the short term at least. Explain this to the class. My experience is that learners will thrive because they know you are trying to do what's best for them. Outline the rationale. The class will realise you have done a 'pre-mortem' and carefully crafted this situation to optimise their experience and outcomes. As a quotation often attributed to Theodore Roosevelt goes, 'Nobody cares how much you know until they know how much you care.' However, this initial arrangement certainly isn't fixed or forever.

Seating plans are in your hands. You lead the learning and alter them depending on the needs of the learners, lesson and outcomes. You are the final arbiter. I have pondered over this, as I am sure many teachers have. Bennett (2020) writes of the 'architecture of attention' and largely that's the key – which configuration is best to optimise learning. Positive moves might be made with the teacher explaining, 'We are making this move because we will be better able to learn if we sit like this.' A clockwork classroom is all about maximising the thinking, learning and participation ratio. The plan might be refined and honed as you get to know the learners – you decide. You reserve the right to direct and have a temporal perspective in mind; everything can be short term.

Sometimes teachers have two plans. One is the *home* seating arrangement, and this can be based on your original 'register routine' configuration. The second option is the *away* seating plan, which can be devised some other way, perhaps based on formative assessment or class dynamics and relationships. Keep it fluid. It's your call, working backwards from intended outcomes.

Sometimes playing 'find your face' can help reduce friction when the away seating is implemented. In this instance, you print out a set of learner thumbnails (do it only once, laminate and keep) and deal these out the way you want learners to sit. To expedite the process, have a prominently displayed 'home' or 'away' sign on the door of the classroom or somewhere highly visible on arrival. This is a non-verbal cue that learners automatically look for leading to a slick lesson start. Many schools have seating plan software such as Class Charts to help with this sort of procedural arrangement so the information can be displayed.

In advance of this, when the class is empty be sure to **sit for a moment in each seat** and check out the view. Try to optimise the experience for everyone. See what the audience experiences as 'learning is optimised when teachers see learning through the eyes of the learner, and when learners see themselves as their own teachers' (Hattie and Yates, 2013). While they don't mean this literally, it's worth checking. If learners are tucked away, around the corner, behind a pillar or close up against the wall, the chances are they won't tell you, and they will hide. They may be in a blind spot or even hidden in plain sight. I have looked closely at what happens in classroom contexts, and I see this all the time, even in classrooms with no obvious obstructions. When I see things like this and film it, the teacher invariably says, 'How did I not realise?' Easy! Because you're juggling a million and one things, including content coverage, instructions, delivery, safety and wellbeing.

It's about a **pre-mortem**. This is vital. My esteemed NQT mentor Jean Wirth told us teaching is like a military campaign: you must anticipate, predict and pre-empt. I guess it's like the hazard perception section of the driver theory test (before my time!). Keep on thinking everything through. James Clear (2018) in his worldwide bestseller talks of a 'failure pre-mortem', so similarly, if you think through why things won't work or go to plan, you can perhaps remove some of the barriers to success in advance. Hopefully these chapters will make you think, provide the shortcuts and help you to avoid some of the traps and pitfalls.

6. A second set of eyes

If you feel you are falling foul of Solomon's Paradox, pair up. King Solomon, considered to be 'the wisest man that ever lived', could help others but not himself. This is a common phenomenon. Teaching can be a very solitary pursuit, and a link between introspection and insight has yet to be found, so a second set of eyes can help. Call on your colleagues as critical friends – those with unmistakeable and unshakeable trustworthiness. In his book *Second Set of Eyes*, Royle (2023) quotes Andy Longley: 'Research from neuroscience tells us the best way to make decisions is in pairs.' Royle goes on to say how individualism can be crippling for you and your organisation.

It is worth noting too that 'happiness is rooted in trust, kindness and social connection' (Gilbert, 2025). The power of benevolence is highlighted in the World Happiness Report 2025. We need to focus on these elements for the happiness of ourselves, our colleagues, the young people we teach and all within the school community.

The goal should be continuous improvement – *kaizen* – as opposed to unattainable perfection. One idea could be a form of reciprocal peer observation (RPO) with a focus on collaborative review. RPO 'focuses on collegial reflection and dialogue based on an equal relationship and mutual learning between the observer and observee' (Ribosa et al., 2023). RPO is strongly supported by international organisations that aim to guide educational change. Its practice is still limited by teachers' resistance to its use, which is why voluntary participation is important for teacher agency and sense of safety (O'Leary and Savage, 2020). A pre-observation meeting clarifies the purpose and allows participants to agree on the scope of the observation. A positive experience can be facilitated through institutional emotional support mechanisms, such as creating time and space for teacher dialogue.

7. Classrooms as an 'elite' context – stadium seating

This approach forms much of my ongoing work in schools. I acted as a 'second set of eyes' for PE teacher Louise Coleman at Glenwood High School in Glenrothes, and from that we developed 'stadium seating' as an idea to help make her classroom more 'clockwork'. Louise had been working with me, having her lessons videoed, and at the start of the lesson and activity transition time we noticed learners splayed out across the sports hall. Louise was straining her voice against the hollowness; the acoustics were awful. It was post-Covid-19, so the need to keep our distance no longer applied, but this learner behaviour seemed to be a hangover from those days. We encouraged learners to break that habit and gather in, but we needed this to be a sea change; something the learners would readily recognise and do automatically, lesson in, lesson out – like clockwork.

So, we chalked a number on the floor for each learner and said that was their place in the 'stadium', as if they were at a match, or the Olympics even! We said we would only be 'showing them to their seats' once, and it was incumbent upon them to remember. The challenge was cranked up. The setting was more realistic because it was linked to a sporting event and we had already generated a sense of occasion. To get the lesson off to a flying start, the learners would reverently take their seats, which added order, rigour, high expectations and early challenge. We had given the sports hall an elite context.

This approach has also worked for Year 1 at Yewdale School in Carlisle, Cumbria. Here the 4-year-olds have their regular carpet spot agreed and sometimes have a special carpet tile or small rug to sit on to publicly acknowledge something that is noteworthy or impressive. Paul Dix (2017) writes about PIP and RIP – praise in public and reprimand in private. Great general guiding principles, although you'll know your learners and some prefer not to have public acknowledgement.

8. Gather and go

In Louise's case, we were formalising a 'gather and go' seating arrangement. This is a staple of science lessons for experiments – think Van der Graaff generator or setting magnesium alight! Similarly, in home economics for showing rubbing in when making pastry, or in design and technology for demonstrating different types of filing. This arrangement potentially has wider applications across the curriculum. Think about when it might benefit your learners to 'gather and go' when you are initially arranging the class theatre style.

The important thing to remember here is that learners are not all going along together at the same time. While sometimes there is a place for this, learners need to ultimately have the opportunity to '*do something* with what they have learned' (Enser, 2025).

Such staggered starts can add fluidity and take account of learners' starting points. You may find you need to set learners off working and then re-gather a small group around you or, better still, around another learner who you know can demonstrate what the others need to know or be able to do. One teacher calls this a 'free workshop', which is a much more enticing prospect than sticking around for extra help! Learners can 'actively engage in their own learning and reflect back on what they have, and have not, learnt and set their own goals' (Enser and Enser, 2020).

You are the final arbiter, but use learners whenever possible – more on this later. You will have learners who can just get on, persevere and work away.

9. Tune in: the importance of listening and quiet time

Daunting as it may sound, some organisations have cracked the code of sustained collaboration. In *Harvard Business Review*, Francesca Gino (2019) writes of observations from Pixar and Webasto, most notably their approaches to raising employees' awareness of fruitful interactions. When Philipp Schramm became Webasto's CFO he introduced a 'Listen like a leader' course with exercises involving asking expansive questions, role play, attentiveness and body language. A focus on the listener, not yourself, with self-checks included.

In successful collaborations, judgement gives way to curiosity. When we really listen our egos and our self-involvement subside, giving everybody the space to understand the situation and one another – and to focus on the mission. The task for teachers is to encourage an outward focus in everyone, challenging the tendency many have to fixate on ourselves and what **we'd** like to say and achieve, instead of what we can learn from others. Jeff Beatty, a program manager, reflected: 'I thought leading was steamrolling people who got in your way – it was about aggressiveness and forcefulness. After going through the class, I can't believe that my wife has put up with me for 30 years' (Gino, 2019).

So, what does this mean for the classroom? Listening can be improved in the classroom initially at a rudimentary level by 'register race', word association and, of course, bingo – the classic listening game.

Think ahead about the subject-specific vocabulary needed for a topic. Be ambitious and make a caller's card (the card you use to keep track of which words have been used) and associated bingo cards using www.myfreebingocards.com. Learners now realise that you prioritise and place emphasis on listening and quiet times, thus minimising distractions. This can be played alongside a series of lessons encouraging curiosity and class discussion. Once a full house is secured learners should be expected to explain the meanings of the words and elaborate upon them, going beyond simple recognition if possible. Learners can even start to question and interrogate each other to deepen substantive and disciplinary understanding. This training can lead into more substantial class contributions, with learners increasingly leading the learning.

When it comes to questioning, listening to the teacher and each other's responses is vital too. More on this in chapter three, section ten.

Varying, most commonly *lowering,* the voice (volume and pitch) can be impactful too. Teacher voices can easily dominate a classroom and become white noise (more on this in chapter six, section five). A clear demarcation between giving your instruction and letting learners get on is important to minimise distraction. Talking while the learners are trying to work either to the whole class or loudly to individuals can reduce 'learners' attentional bandwidth' (McCrea quoted in Clark, 2024). Try to be mindful of this. In my experience, this is the number-one change made by teachers following videoed lessons. It's stark when seen and heard on film. Practising the economy of our language is important. Think too about when you can perhaps use a different voice, a recording, a colleague and, of course, the learners – this is when you'll hear a pin drop!

10. Word up: etymology and morphology

The Oxford Language Report 2023–24 makes for depressing reading: 'Fewer than 3 in 10 teachers report using any specific vocabulary-building programmes' although 'broadening learners' vocabulary is a "medium" to "high" strategic priority in 90% of schools. … There's a lot of intent but a lack of interconnected implementation' (Oxford University Press, 2024). The report recommends an aligned approach between home and school, the aim being to close the 'word gap' between the vocabulary learners have at their fingertips and what they need to access their education. Dedicated tools like glossaries can be used to expose learners to the new words needed, and these could be shared with parents and carers. High expectations and emphasis on using these subject-specific words at home and in class can lead to a greater understanding and a more 'clockwork' classroom, whereby learners regulate themselves and each other. They have their checklist of vocabulary at the ready. This is commonplace in MFL (modern foreign languages) lessons, but we all have our distinct disciplinary words that learners must have access to. Incentives like register wars, bingo and word association mean words are revisited so that confidence and fluency may follow.

Developing a language-loving community can be done in part by exploring the etymology – the origin of words and the historical development of their meanings. This unlocks stories and deepens understanding. One way to avoid missed chances is for teachers to come together and pool their vocabulary to see where reinforcement can occur, so learners can transfer their understanding between contexts. Similarly, morphemes (the smallest unit of language) like prefixes (e.g. geo-, trans-, ultra-, tele-, extra-, over-) or suffixes (e.g. -tion, -ness, -ion, -able, -ment, -ful, -less, -archy, -icide) are important in phonics in both reading and spelling, as well as vocabulary and comprehension. If learners are familiar with these, they may well carry the mental models and shared language with them along the corridor and up the stairs to the next lesson – clockwork! This relies on teacher reinforcement and the power of departmental teaching teams to identify and deconstruct the words learners encounter throughout the curriculum and then share them. A classic example is precipitate/precipitation, which is encountered in some form in MFL, geography, environmental science, geology, English and history. If learners have a deeper understanding of the meaning of the words (to cast down, headlong, hastily) their understanding across the curriculum will be reinforced.[4]

11. Running records

Another Jean Wirth special was the suggestion to keep a running record of notable things learners said or did. She told us NQTs to do this from day one. At our weekly meetings she asked us to recount the best classroom event of the week. She stated that although your learners will be learning from you, preserving a place for what you learn from and about your learners is essential. This time to reflect and emphasise the positive reaps dividends.

Making this capturing the treasures a habit really helped me with the clockwork nature of lessons. It meant I was more with it, in that I increasingly knew about learners' strengths, referred to them, reinforced them and played to them. It was a preventative and proactive strategy seeming to dispel any possible negativity in terms of learning dispositions or troublesome behaviour because expectations were held high. Jacob Kounin has written about 'with-it-ness' and the 'Ripple Effect',[5] and I felt I experienced this. Being a step ahead seemed to add to my credibility as a relatively new recruit. Because learners knew I was taking account, they simply became more accountable.

David Didau calls this kind of note-making 'messy markbooks', and it's exactly that.[6] For some more orderly folk, this could be an app on an iPad or a clipboard in hand; each to their own. It suits me because I am messy, and my markbook would be a mass of notes squeezed in here and there to monitor participation in and across lessons.

In addition, perhaps have the learners' faces printed out or available elsewhere as postage-stamp-sized profiles. I deliberately placed this section further into the chapter to emphasise the ongoing cumulative nature of learner intel gathering. The situation for learners can change: they are growing, maturing and changing as we all are, and often responding to

---

4   Lindsay Bruce at OUP developed this great resource for history in 2019 https://fdslive.oup.com/www.oup.com/oxed/Closing_the_Word_Gap_-_history.pdf?region=uk and for a more general resource, see www.marymyatt.com/blog/help-to-close-the-word-gap.

5   For more, see https://en.wikibooks.org/wiki/Classroom_Management_Theorists_and_Theories/Jacob_Kounin.

6   You can read about messy markbooks in David's 20 January 2024 blog at learningspy.co.uk.

life events. It's therefore important to be vigilant and continue to gather evidence, noticing any changes that might require a different approach. This way we constantly remain ambitious for learners (which, since you are reading this book, you clearly are!) and strive to work out how best to unlock and nurture their ongoing potential.

12. MEOW

One approach that might work for learners who perhaps need some extra motivation is a MEOW – Minimum Expected OWtcome (sic). Allow me to explain.

I have taught several learners over the years who, for various reasons, have been reluctant to push themselves to do more or aim higher. After much agonising I decided initially to put a little pencil mark in their book and suggest they tried to work up to the line. It worked to some extent, but in all honesty during the cut and thrust of lessons I often forgot to return to it to check. Some learners weren't that bothered. I suspect the pencil mark hadn't exactly captivated them! I realised that learners often respond best to visuals, particularly pets or animals. Since I have very rudimentary drawing skills, I drew a cat as a MEOW, the idea being that this was the Minimum Expected OWtcome (sic). This unlocked a whole new level of enthusiasm. This time the learners loved it and were motivated to come to me and show me what they had done. The little cat propelled them, and they started setting targets for themselves and each other.

The MFL department at Pendle Vale College in Nelson, Lancashire, christened this 'chase the cat' (*courir après le chat*) with learners telling the teacher in French that they had caught the cat. I ended up getting a cat stamp since the idea seemed to cultivate a desire to aim high with learners increasingly regulating themselves – clockwork!

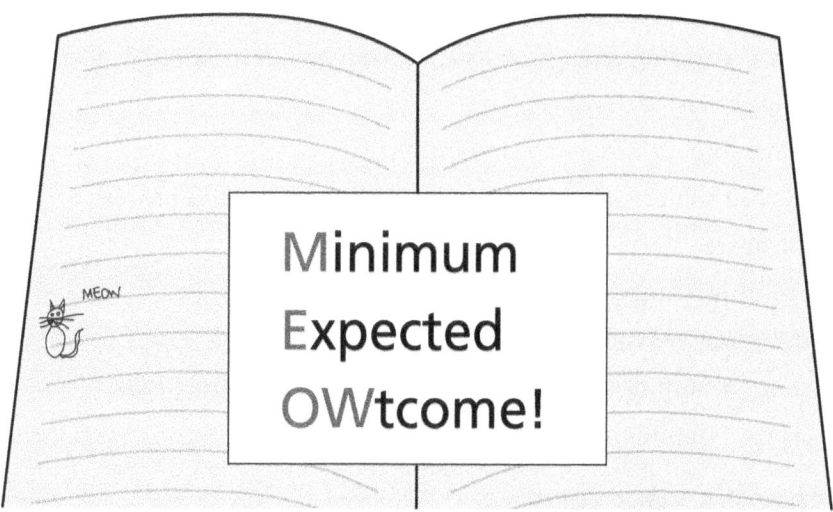

Minimum
Expected
OWtcome!

Wherever I have shared the approach, it has been a success. It has both primary and high school application. I have come across several alternative examples. Art teacher Gaynor Davies at Portobello High School in Edinburgh draws a wrapped sweetie and her learners aim for the candy. She calls it 'Keep it Sweet!' Rachel Benn, a probationary maths teacher in Scotland, draws a star and encourages learners to 'Reach!' At the Gillford Centre Pupil Referral Unit in Carlisle one teacher adopted a 'Make me smile' smiley emoji, which had transformative effects in terms of the quantity of written English work produced by learners of both primary and secondary age. Increased staying power, perseverance and motivation was notable. I am so heartened to have seen and be able to share these examples with you. The little strategy obviously has wide appeal. Maybe you could give it a go in your setting?

Teachers are brilliant. I hope you will take away, run with and customise these ideas. Perhaps document and share them with your colleagues. Best of all, let me know what you have done and share your triumphs (hopefully) with me.

Takeaways – high expectations are the key to successful outcomes

- Do (and keep doing) your learner research.
- Make overt your ways of committing information to memory.

- Insist on routine gap-closing.
- Ensure seating arrangements are driven by a desired end goal.
- Collaborate with others.
- Give your classroom an elite context.
- Revisit subject-specific words; learning is an iterative process.
- Staggered starts.
- Value listening and quiet time.
- Emphasise etymology.
- Keep a running record of learner intel to remain ambitious.
- Have a minimum expected outcome in mind.

Now it's your turn

- Use the template on page 102 to have a go at some of the 12 strategies that underpin the principle of 'high expectations'.
- Remember to persevere in order to make it routine.
- Set yourself one or more intentions and pledge to review your ongoing progress.

Recommended reading

- *Teaching One-Pagers Volume 1* – Jamie Clark.
- *Teaching One-Pagers Volume 2* – Jamie Clark.
- *Essential Motivation in the Classroom*, second edition – Ian Gilbert.
- *Bjork and Bjork's Desirable Difficulties in Action* – Jade Pearce and Isaac Moore.

Chapter 2 map

Set your stall out

1	What's your lesson soundtrack?
2	Businesslike and purposeful space
3	Shelf help, help yourself
4	Slicker with a clicker
5	Replicate the resource
6	Be discerning

Chapter 2:
Set your stall out

'The environment is the invisible hand that shapes human behaviour.'
James Clear, Atomic Habits, *2018*

The quote above from *Atomic Habits* helps us think about use of space as a cognitive resource. We can all relate, I'm sure; if the biscuits are handy, we might be more inclined to tuck in. If the trainers are by the front door, we might be more likely to put them on – here's hoping! This resonated with me, and I realised there had been meticulous care taken around classroom set-up where lessons were calm, orderly and running smoothly. Norms, routines and habits were firmly in place, teachers had high expectations, and learners had high expectations of themselves and each other. Tacit understandings had been established, and the environment had been designed for success. Rather like a clock mechanism, the interconnected pieces had been delicately assembled so that power was transferred to the learners. There was much more learner self-regulation and independence than in classrooms where this had not been explicitly set out.

Habit building requires perseverance; it is all too easy to give up if a routine or desired effect doesn't take hold straight away. James Clear calls this a 'valley of disappointment'. Mastery requires practice. We often expect progress to be linear, but the reality is that things become slicker with time, and it is only in the future we realise the value of the previous work we have done. However, the work is not wasted. It is being stored until later when the true value of previous effort is revealed. To make a meaningful difference, habits need to break through what Clear calls the 'plateau of latent potential'. He suggests forgetting about goals and focusing on the systems and processes that lead to those results.

In classrooms I observed where a teacher had clearly thought about the systems and overtly 'set their stall out', learners were being nudged in the right direction. Behavioural science suggests that making positive change easier and more tempting is more likely to yield results. There was a lightness of touch and a fruitful compounding of habits. Adult experts manage their use of space as a problem-solving resource. Through careful planning of space, a considerable amount of cognitive offloading is achieved (for more on cognitive offloading, see chapter six, section six).

We see this daily; Amazon have had such success (whether you like it or not) since they succeeded in minimising the clicks required to make a purchase. This means that we are potentially more inclined to revert to using them to expedite the buying process. Amazon has doubled its global Prime subscriber base since early 2018, from 100 million to over 200 million worldwide. Habits have been formed; friction has been reduced. What can we take away from this for use in the classroom?

Removing obstacles that inhibit learner progress and creating the conditions for them to meet their own needs makes learners more likely to be productive – a 'more carrot, less stick' approach. This chapter offers some tried-and-tested suggestions for setting success in motion. Have a read, review your situation, and if there are takeaways, specify the change and commit to action using the 'have a go' template at the back of the book.

1. What's your lesson soundtrack?

Your classroom can be full of sounds that distract your learners and slow down progress. There are a few techniques in this section that can quieten your lesson soundtrack and improve conditions so that your learners can make the most of your lesson.

Non-verbal cues

Non-verbal cues make lessons slick. It's commonplace for teachers to make signs or hand gestures to direct learners. For instance, fingers on lips to reduce noise or pointing to the bin for litter. Be aware that some learners may find it difficult to read non-verbal cues, so they may require explicit teaching. Be sure to check for understanding. The amount of reminding and persistence required will of course depend on your context. I doubt we will ever crack it, as we are dealing with human beings after all, not robots (thank goodness!). But sometimes shooting a knowing glance can do the trick once expectations are more embedded. Building this learner automaticity means lessons can be richer in terms of content – more focused, businesslike and purposeful. One way of doing this is by having everything accessible, available to see or hear as appropriate. This frees you up to engage in subject-specific conversations, so the soundtrack of the lesson involves listening and responding positively to complexity, stories and problem-solving, thereby deepening understanding and moving learners on.

A fabulous example comes from Dr Ian Barker, chemistry teacher at Trinity School, Carlisle. When learners arrived at his classroom, he found (like many of us) that he was repeating the same procedural instructions over and over again. In his case it referred to textbook pages. On arrival, he'd be saying, 'Please turn to pages 150–151.' During a filmed lesson we tallied several counts of this and realised he could set his stall out more clearly. Ian decided to affix a laminated A3 board to his wall that read 'Today's textbook pages are ...' (rather like how hymn numbers are displayed in some places of worship). The pages could be displayed daily and rubbed off for the next class.

Learners now come into the classroom (I've seen it first-hand), look over to the A3 board, silently get the information they need and make a quicker, quieter, self-sufficient start. This allows Dr Barker to meet and greet his learners, continue to build relationships and further cement the unconditional positive regard he has for his learners. He can amplify what is important. Similarly, he could enjoy a 'cordial silence', a principle of Zen Buddhist teaching and golden in a classroom (Masuno, 2022). It's removing the need to talk for the sake of talking.

In Dr Barker's lab the context has become the cue, and social influence has meant most learners automatically now look to the board on arrival. When some learners initially began to do this, Dr Barker celebrated it by providing positive feedback to reinforce this self-regulation: 'Excellent Natasha, I noticed you looked straight at the board to see what pages you needed in the textbook.' In this way the feedback was specific, immediate and directly linked to self-regulation, and therefore more likely to move learning forwards as outlined as a recommendation in the Education Endowment Foundation Feedback Report 2021.[7] This is opposed to more personal feedback, which is less likely to move learners on since they are unclear specifically about what they are good at. For instance, 'Well done, you're a born chemist' is pretty meaningless in terms of offering anything concrete that learners can go on to repeat.

In this way Dr Barker has nudged his learners in the right direction by making change easy and tempting. The unnecessary focus on extraneous information has stopped. This consideration of the role of working memory reduces cognitive load and optimises intellectual performance, so learners place mental emphasis upon what is important. Harry Fletcher-Wood (2021) writes how persuasion and enforcement aren't always enough to overcome obstacles and emotions. Motivation fluctuates. Competency is motivational, and so success and learning are the best goals. In this case it's a quick win. The critical mass of learners has been won over. Learners arrive and are automatically now ready to start – clockwork!

Dr Barker nominated a learner to write up the page numbers on arrival and/or rub them off at the end of the lesson to prepare for the next group. This daring to devolve or delegate to learners whenever possible is the focus of chapter three. It's another development to maximise wins by classroom 'habit stacking' as outlined in *Atomic Habits* (Clear, 2018). It also means the change is made 'by' learners, leading to greater buy in. They are included in the system improvement (Fletcher-Wood, 2021) so that rather than an idea being imposed upon them, they have a stake in the interconnected mechanism.

I have seen this approach replicated with recipe pages in home economics lessons, Spanish pages in MFL and recently in maths at Glenrothes High School, which included the page number and the relevant equipment. The curriculum subject is immaterial, but it will be a helpful approach for you when setting your stall out.

---

7   See pp. 22–23 of 'Teacher feedback to improve pupil learning: Guidance report'. Available at: https://educationendowmentfoundation.org.uk/.

If you don't have a single teaching base and perhaps work across multiple rooms this technique is less easy to execute, but if there was a 'Today's textbook pages are ...' template set up in departmental rooms as standard, the shared language and consistency would be there.

These visual and non-verbal cues enable the 'soundtrack' of the lesson to be subject-specific. Think about what learners hear in your lesson: if it's procedural classroom management talk then it's not furthering the learning. If you're constantly repeating the name of an inattentive learner, again, that is what your attentive learners will hear and remember. 'Stephen, Stephen, Stephen...' I doubt it's GCSE 'Stephen' they have come to study! Keep it content-based as far as possible. Talk quietly to individuals if needs be. There is a lot to be said for reprimand in private and praise in public (RIP and PIP) (Dix, 2017). Learners really do appreciate that in my experience. Sometimes even praise in *private* might be valued more once you know your learners. Some are modest, discreet and do not like any attention or fuss. It's always best to ask learners about their preferences – beware of assuming!

Similarly, not everybody needs to be reprimanded. Avoid your blind spots and think who specifically you need to speak to. It isn't easy at times but whole-class awareness is vital, as is the need to prevent antagonising learners who might feel unfairly treated if caught in the crossfire of something else. Accentuate the positive.

Nurture targets

At St Thomas Aquinas there are regularly changing nurture targets – reminder messages with an underlying focus on growth mindset displayed on classroom doors. The initial lesson slide is a reminder about routines and expectations. Again, these nudge learners into creating the optimal conditions for learning. Judicious use of this approach can prevent a teacher becoming white noise with needless repetition of instructions. This can sadly become a feature of classrooms when information and instructions lose impact at best or are totally ignored at worst.

Another nudge I have seen to encourage good manners and consideration are stickers on doors in classrooms and corridors reminding learners to be aware of others who might need the door held open for them, thus building a habit. As my old Nanna used to say, 'It's nice to be nice!'

Mobile phones

The thorny issue of mobile phones in schools has generated huge debate. They may be a thing of the past in classrooms by the time you read this. Updated guidance was issued by the DfE in January 2026 with case studies of how to implement a mobile-free school environment. Screen time can displace positive activities and one in five children has experienced online bullying.

In Scotland the growing challenges are recognised, and government guidance empowers headteachers to implement policies as they see fit. A routine that works very well in many schools (notably at Mearns Castle High School, East Renfrewshire) is that of a phone box. On arrival in class, learners place their phones in a teacher-controlled safety deposit box, and these exist in every room of the school. I've also seen pouches and wooden phone-holder stands with multiple numbered slots, and 'phone hotels' where each learner is issued with a number and the corresponding slot is where the learner's phone resides for the duration of the lesson or day. The growing implementation of one-to-one devices is increasingly removing the need for mobiles when using apps in lessons. This topic will most likely be everchanging as technology changes, so be sure to keep on top of new developments!

2. Businesslike and purposeful space

Having the classroom looking as orderly as possible sends a message that the lesson is the priority. So for a clockwork start, the environment needs to have been cared for by the outgoing learners: board cleaned, chairs under tables and litter gone. This engenders clarity and prevents any confusion. In busy schools with shared classrooms and part-time working, if this isn't done routinely it can cause unnecessary stress. I liken it to a restaurant; you wouldn't be impressed if the place was a tip with mucky plates left over from the last diners. The same principle applies to your classroom; ensure it is welcoming, purposeful, businesslike and expecting learning!

My own desk and history cupboard (as my colleagues will happily testify!) were always famously chaotic but the space that the learners arrived in never was – as far as I could realistically manage. As a department we had shared expectations of what a good one looked like (WAGOLL) regarding the appearance of the room. In addition to our agreed minimum standards, we often liaised with each other (we had 12 members of staff in the department at one point). For instance, if the next class needed tables and chairs in a particular configuration, it was part of the deal at the end. I'd say, 'Mr Hurst's class needs the tables in five groups of six, let's sort it!' Then it would be all hands on deck to make it happen. This exchange requires communication and awareness about what colleagues are doing, a shared understanding and shared goals about smooth lessons and consistency. This give-and-take and being aware of each other's starting points was what helped us to function well; the power of the team. As the head of department, I wanted consistency and for learners to receive the best deal – high standards and expectations, regardless of the individuality of the teacher they had. The same goes for high-quality resources, as far as money allows. Clean mini-whiteboards (learners get very excited about this), pens that work (woohoo!) and high-quality, clear, appealing resources. Scrappy, dog-eared textbooks, for instance, send a slipshod message.

It is well documented that there can be huge variations along the same corridor if a consistent approach and expectations don't apply. Liaise with colleagues to share the load. Although I rail against the idea of non-negotiation, we had a shared understanding that the environment would be left as we would like to find it. Ms Edwards at St Thomas Aquinas in Glasgow does this: she has reminders on the monitor and by the light switch about how things should be left. Teaching shouldn't be a solitary pursuit. It's a team game for the learners, and it's much healthier if it's a team game for you and your colleagues too. As Bill Walton said, 'Winning is about having the whole team on the same page' (quoted in Crome, 2023).

3. Shelf help, help yourself

Say this one in your best Sean Connery voice!

Make learner self-regulation the norm, have a help shelf, helpdesk, inspiration station or enable table. Call it what you will, or somewhere digital if that's how you're operating. Essentially, this is a repository for all that is needed for the lesson and beyond. Shape it with your learners. Talk to them about what helps them pursue success and whet their appetites for more.

Trust your learners to help themselves, and provide the information so they can select what suits them. Some teachers might recoil from this learner movement, but being too reliant on you leads to increased wait time, breeds neediness and is ultimately counterproductive. More on 'dare to devolve' in chapter three. A working wall is a good starting point where learners can access information and may not have to move from their seats, but the information needs to be highly visible for this to work. I have seen this used to great effect in Ms Peebles' drama lesson at St Mungo's in Glasgow. Often in primary schools learners are trusted to move around, and then in secondary they are confined to their seats, arguably being de-skilled! We can learn from cross-phase colleagues and through-schools, which often have a more seamless arrangement. Like most things, if the routine is started young it is more likely to stick and become the norm.

At Yewdale Primary School, Carlisle, classrooms have helpdesks with, for example, multiplication squares, pens, pencils, rulers, rubbers, sharpeners, colours, paper, two seats and a toy phone where Year 4s can take a friend to help them explain or go over something. It's a mock-up 'phone a friend' idea offering a beneficial paired opportunity. Teachers give feedback directly, encouraging this self-regulation, which is therefore more impactful. For instance, 'Niamh is doing the right thing there by using the dictionary to check the spelling of that word,' which is much more likely to propel learning forwards than 'Well done, Niamh'. However, beware of being patronising – the age of the learners matters in terms of the kind of advice given (see EEF, 2021).

This is not to say learners aren't routinely bringing their own equipment to lessons – in most cases they are. This is of course an organisational skill and habit to be encouraged. The Mearns Castle maths department use more show than tell here, so learners see precisely what is expected of them in terms of which maths equipment to bring. A classroom visual displays exactly what is required as a constant reminder so learners can set their own stall out.

The need for glossaries is something I have increasingly become aware of when setting up helpdesks. I was working with mathematicians at Park Hall Academy, and the teacher had created what I thought was a dream helpdesk. After talking to some learners, they said although the desk had lots of equipment, there was no way they could they find out how to distinguish between *solve*, *simplify* or *substitute*. I realised the maths helpdesk was missing a subject-specific glossary. Ask learners what would be beneficial for them. It could be rulers or guides for reading to keep everyone together, numbering lines, blocks of text, worked examples, multiplication squares or even subject-specific magazines to enthuse and inspire. I've seen *BBC History Magazine*, *National Geographic* and various design magazines used to great effect in this regard at Madras College, St Andrews.

'Stuckness' routines are another way of developing positive attitudes, skills and habits. David Bones at William Howard School asked his learners from age 11 to 18 how they would solve problems in maths. They told him their suggested approaches, and the composite responses were made into a poster that was then displayed in all classrooms.

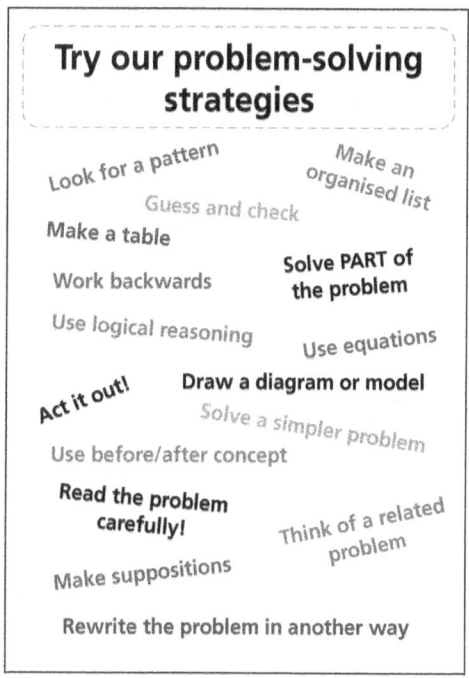

Because the ideas were generated by the learners, the whole process was done *by* them not *to* them, therefore encouraging learner buy-in. The ideas are randomly arranged on the poster to take account of the fact that they aren't hierarchical. We are all different so a learner can select something from the varied suggestions that might work for them and give it a try. Diversity is catered for and choices are offered, which is motivational. Learners used to say, 'There's no point asking you for help, sir, you'll just tap the poster!' Up to a point this was very true; he wanted them to at least try to find their own way forwards, thus preventing overreliance on the teacher.

QR codes can also point learners in the right direction. They can link to explainer videos, translations or audio files. A teacher at Lanercost Primary School used this technique to 'speak' maths problems to her Year 1 learners. They scanned the QR code with an iPad and, although some weren't able to read, they followed the words alongside hearing what was required, and they could reply to it as needed. This can also help with literacy and be beneficial for EAL learners.

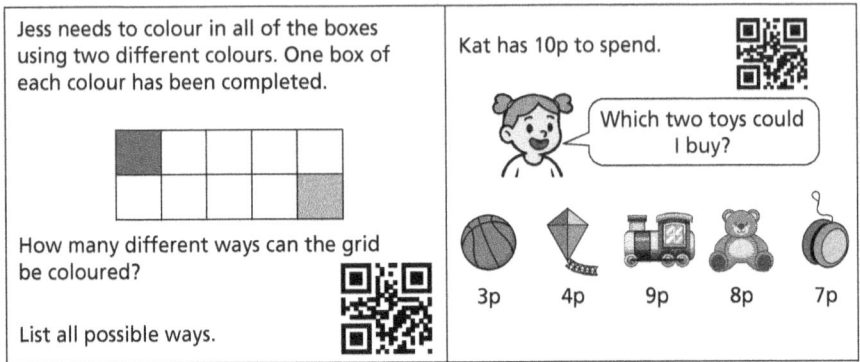

4. Slicker with a clicker

'Next slide please!' Can you remember this request during the UK Covid-19 briefings by Sir Chris Whitty? Forget that! Get a digital presenter clicker. This really is an easy game changer. Physics teacher and pastoral leader Mr Hale at St Thomas Aquinas school in Glasgow tells me he's a new man now that he's roaming around the room with a clicker! His step count has gone up too. Win–win! A clicker frees you up and enables you to be among the learners. It means in terms of presenting you can be slicker with animations and reveals, adding intrigue and jeopardy, allowing you to adjust the challenge in real time. It may help you to have a greater awareness of cognitive load if you stand deeper in the classroom, seeing it as part of the audience – what the learners see. A clicker can allow more opportunity for targeted questioning, checking of starting points, dynamism and generally detecting learning. It's a liberating piece of kit and if it has a pointer, better still!

The alternative is you having to repeatedly retreat to the laptop or be confined to the desk. This prevents you from moving around or from activating and challenging your learners (as appropriate). It can slow the pace of the lesson and mean you are not as vigilant, which can reduce learner accountability, lead to disengagement and create further problems.

There are also various apps that can turn your smartphone into a clicker for a remote classroom projector – even more reason to be sure the learners' phones are safely out of reach in the phone box! A few points to keep in mind:

- Projector manufacturer's apps provide remote-control functionality via Wi-Fi, provided both the phone and the projector are on the same network.

- Presentation software apps like Canva have remotes that allow the advancing of slides via QR codes.

- When using general projector remote apps, connectivity, compatibility and network restrictions are all key considerations. In my experience, a separate USB-activated clicker works well.

5. Replicate the resource

Something else to think about is the location of the information relative to the learners. If your information is only on a central screen, there is a chance that is not proximal enough for learners to fully interact with. Few learners admit when they can't see something in lessons as they often do not want to create a fuss or draw attention to themselves. Choice is best. Do not assume everyone can see the board. Close the gap before it arises. Offer handouts to make sure the content is more immediate. Have these routinely available on the helpdesk so learners can easily and quietly be self-selecting in terms of what works for them. I know there is a photocopying cost, but if learners can't access the information, they are impeded in the lesson. Offering handouts is also useful for learners who find it difficult to look up at a board, read, track and process.

When it comes to learners attending to the task in hand, this idea of replicating can avoid a learning pitfall. In this case, the pitfall is the distraction of the information being remote. Remove the distraction so learners can study with full focus (Harvard, 2025).

Some schools are lucky enough to have one-to-one devices or iPads, in which case the learners can be up close and personal with the material, but if not, it is wise to give the option. The late Mr Ritson, head of SEND at St Aidan's, gave me this advice very early on in my career, and it has stuck with me.

When filming lessons I have seen all sorts of permutations. Mixed economies work well in class, where perhaps 50% of learners look at the screen and 50% choose to have something closer. Learners can mix and match according to individual need. We are all different, and isn't that marvellous! Be aware of divergence and the need to facilitate what will optimise learner outcomes and enable learners to increasingly, independently reach their potential. One of my incredible GCSE students with sight issues sat at the front with A3 resources, and we made an A3 version of the textbook (don't tell the publishers!). Remember, not everyone is the same as or learns in the same way as you.

6. Be discerning

Finally, this is a short section – be discerning. There, I have said it. It is so important.

It's not easy but it is certainly something to be mindful of. If one learner needs help, it doesn't mean everybody does! Beware the tendency to let the tail wag the dog. If a teacher sees one person struggling or making a mistake, it's often followed by, 'Right everybody, pens down!' (Sound familiar?) There is nothing more infuriating for those who are getting on beautifully. So, ask yourself, 'Who *actually* needs help? Who needs a reset?' Rarely is it everybody. This is the point that probably arises the most often when reviewing lessons. Be sure to set yourself up as the teacher who can make distinctions; read the room and don't fall into the trap of being swept along. This nuanced approach is powerful. Learners know you are on to them as **individuals**. You don't simply see the class as a homogenous mass; you know their singular activities, as far as possible.

Similarly, avoid thoughts like 'this is a tricky class' because again the individuals are lost in such a sweeping generalisation. Try to visualise and think about the learners separately. Step back and take a broader look. It's most likely that not everybody needs to be reprimanded.

Be sure to let the learners know that you know them as individuals; use their names and vary them for positive purposes. Take a beat and develop your class awareness. Move around the room to maintain vigilance and increase questioning. I tend to purposefully look to the four corners of the classroom, the outlying areas, and make a point of including those learners. This isn't straightforward. Most teachers tend to focus on the middle of the room, so it requires a bit of deliberate practice, but it's something to at least be mindful of.

Also try to think, 'Who can I use to help a learner out rather than intervening immediately myself?' Put learners in touch with **each other** at times if appropriate to build that culture of support. Avoid having learners waiting for you to run around the classroom as the sole provider of information and support. Build classroom camaraderie. Know about individual strengths. Stepping back a little can be a strange habit to get into at first. It involves letting go of control which some of us don't find easy, but I encourage you to try it. Build 'stuckness' routines like 'C3B4Me' (see three before me), where learners must seek out three sources of help before defaulting to the teacher. For instance, learners might:

- Look back through their book.

- Consult a friend.

- Use the helpdesk before calling upon the teacher.

By encouraging this you are building independence and self-reliance – important lifelong skills.

Takeaways – optimise outcomes with classroom design

- Use non-verbal cues when you can to keep the talk on topic.

- Maintain high standards; keep the classroom environment businesslike and purposeful.

- Actively encourage learners to show independence in helping themselves and each other.

- Be more efficient by using a clicker.

- Offer handouts.

- Maintain whole-class awareness. See the bigger picture and avoid being disproportionately swayed by individual learners.

Now it's your turn

- Use the template on page 102 to have a go at some of the six strategies that underpin the principle of 'setting your stall out'.

- Remember to persevere in order to make it routine.

- Set yourself one or more intentions and pledge to review your ongoing progress.

Recommended reading

- *Atomic Habits* – James Clear.

Chapter 3 map
Dare to devolve

1	The value of delegating – issue the jobs
2	Starting points
3	Experts in the room
4	Study buddies
5	Home helps
6	Pass the pen
7	Spotlight on the students
8	Flo's feedback
9	Prop it up
10	Avoid repetition
11	Activating and challenging

Chapter 3:
Dare to devolve

'We can't directly teach dispositions, we must enculturate them.'
Ritchhart, 2023

One of my Year 9s once told me, 'Mr Wilson is really in control of his class, because he lets us take charge.' Initially, this might sound terrifyingly counterintuitive, but it is worth unpicking. What the learner meant here was that Mr Wilson (head of sixth form, well-respected, long-serving, expert RE teacher) was daring to judiciously devolve. He was placing trust in his learners by allowing a measure of autonomy. By delegating, in a sense, he was even more able to conduct or orchestrate what was taking place to optimise classroom outcomes.

This idea could unnerve some teachers who like to keep control, but please read on. Some reflexive thinking might be required here whereby you critically examine your own feelings, reactions, assumptions and behaviours to understand how this influences what you do or think in the classroom. I realise this is not necessarily easy. Nonetheless, see what you might be able to take from this chapter depending on your own starting point.

It might be important to note that in 2024, UK 15-year-olds were sadly at the bottom of a European satisfaction league, with 25% reporting low life satisfaction, compared to 7% of Dutch children of the same age. When asked to rate how happy they felt about 10 aspects of life, school came out lowest. The Good Childhood Report 2024 by the Children's Society (Booth, 2024b) highlights that girls and those children from disadvantaged backgrounds are particularly affected, and the decline in wellbeing is linked to the Covid-19 pandemic, rising poverty, concerns over safety, the climate emergency, and other stresses and strains that prevent a happy and fulfilled childhood. Dutch teenagers ranked as among the happiest in the world for several years, with teachers who are not authoritarian but accept high levels of learner self-determination.

Mr Wilson (in a large, mixed, inner-city state comprehensive) interacted with learners in a way that supported collaboration and responsible risk-taking, rather than command and control. He was modelling the habits of an effective learner, so the learners didn't see him as a pre-formed expert. He was respecting and valuing their contributions as thinkers and learners. The lesson was seen as a collective enterprise. There were opportunities for learners to display agency, pursue passions, show their knowledge and skills, embrace roles and become increasingly empowered self-directed learners. The learners were experiencing 'flow' in the lessons. This is a state of mind with high challenge and low stress, as written about by Mihaly Csikszentmihalyi (**cheek**-sent-me-**high**-ee). Look it up in *Flow: The Psychology of Happiness*. It all sounds great in theory, but how does it work in practice? Here are some techniques you might find useful to help you do the same.

1. The value of delegating – issue the jobs

Teaching can be utterly relentless. From the meeting and greeting as the learners arrive at your door, you are on duty, so think about what roles you can give away to preserve your voice and energy levels, and free you up to chat about non-procedural issues. Apologies in advance – your step count will drop but your stress level might too! Think of the door, windows, blinds, lights, resources – figure out who can do what to save you a job. Again, it's about making this a routine.

Formalise it and issue roles and responsibilities, and perhaps mention this in school reports. For instance, 'Jen made our lessons run smoothly this year because she was in charge of technical support.' In my experience, many learners thrive on this responsibility and genuinely embrace it. It runs alongside high expectations and the fact that learners are being relied upon to play a role as part of the team.

Some teachers might need to practise delegation. It's hard to let go of control. We feel responsible for the outcome and are aware that the task needs to be done right. We often focus on the short-term goal rather than the long-term system of developing others through delegation. We favour getting the job done fast over the reasons for delegating, allowing others to feel engaged and to grow, and allowing ourselves more time in the long run.

Doug Lemov said, 'Understanding and feeling connected to a purpose not only makes people happier, it also makes them feel more connected and trusted' (quoted in Crome, 2023). I quite agree, and while in this instance it is being applied to adults, in my experience it applies to young people too. I have seen from Reception up to higher education the positive value of giving learners roles and responsibilities. Playing a part for the collective good links back to a tribal, club mentality. One primary school I worked at in London had Year 5 and 6 learners meeting and greeting, taking coats, organising refreshments – on occasion, even answering the phone! We should beware of underestimating young people and think about the adults we would like them to become.

An MFL teacher I worked with in Bury, Lancashire had a class of 27 learners and nine classroom jobs that needed to be done. She made nine job cards and dealt them out alongside 18 blanks. Learners initially had a one in three chance of getting a role, which they carried out for three weeks. Then she shuffled the cards again and repeated the process. In this case, as well as the usual roles for distribution of materials, she also had learners responsible for making announcements in the target language (French or Spanish), organising transitions, countdowns and cheerleading. It was very impressive. This was done from the very first lesson, enculturating and empowering individual class members. The learners stepped up and were leading the learning.

In a project-based situation with a class of exclusively 15- and 16-year-old males, I saw a very slick operation. As learners arrived at a lesson, the teacher issued each with an A5 clipboard with tasks for that day attached. It was likened to a workplace setting with a career focus, which gave meaning. Allocating timescales, high expectations and self-regulation all led to an arrangement whereby work was completed and tasks accomplished. Tick boxes were added to give that sense of satisfaction and completion.

2. Starting points

Checking on learners' starting points is vital. If you don't routinely do this, please make it part of your practice. Noted American psychologist David Ausubel working in the field of cognitive science (McLeod, 2024) said, 'The most important single factor influencing learning is what the learner already knows.' According to Ausubel, new information is incorporated into existing hierarchically organised schemata. New information is added or subsumed and can only occur where similarities and links are found between past concepts and new ones. To achieve meaningful learning and retention, teachers should activate learners' prior knowledge so that they can more easily make connections between what they are learning and what they already know (Clark, 2024). The need to recognise learners' unique 'learning fingerprints' was emphasised by Graham Nuthall in his groundbreaking work *The Hidden Lives of Learners* (Kara, 2025).

Before teaching new information, it's important to gauge what learners already know by warming them up and bringing existing knowledge to mind. Facilitating paired talk to make predictions, ask questions and verbalise existing understanding, preconceptions and/or misconceptions makes learning more meaningful.

Carl Hendrick posted on X that '"knowing" is not binary, it's not an on/off thing', which reminds us that we move through stages – hearing, recognising, recalling and mastering – before knowledge becomes truly useable. See the useful table below of learners' 'knowing' words from Beck, McKeown and Kucan (2013).

Stage 1: Never saw it before.	No knowledge.
Stage 2: Heard it, but don't know what it means.	General sense; for example, mendacious has a negative connotation.
Stage 3: Recognizes it in context as having something to do with _____ .	Narrow, context-bound knowledge. Has knowledge of a word but not able to recall it readily enough to use in appropriate situation.
Stage 4: Knows it well.	Rich, decontextualized knowledge of a word's meaning, its relationship to other words, and its extension to metaphorical uses.

Walking chocolate bar

One great low-stakes way of detecting learners' starting points and allowing them to absorb new information while interacting with each other is 'walking chocolate bar'. This is a technique popularised by Isabella Wallace and Leah Kirkman (2014) in their book *Talk-Less Teaching*.

The idea is that learners take a piece of A4 paper (a coloured sheet adds some novelty value) and fold it into eight equal sections to replicate chunks of a chocolate bar. No real chocolate is involved in this activity – sadly! The unfurled paper can then be used in various ways. I tend to give learners around 60 seconds to jot down different words, concepts or ideas

– maybe even pictures or emojis – that they associate with the topic in the various boxes. This represents their starting point.

1. Learners fold paper to create eight boxes (or more if required).

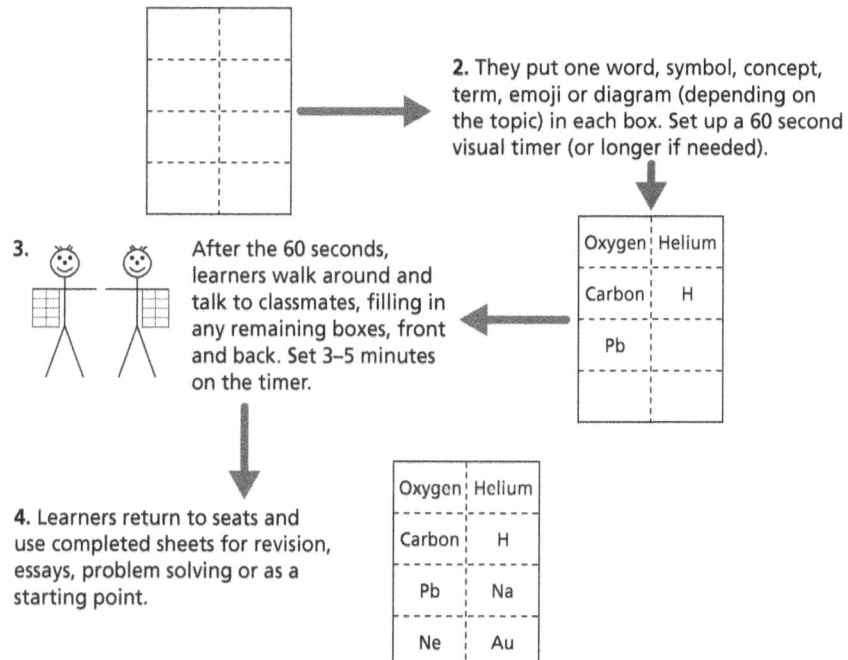

2. They put one word, symbol, concept, term, emoji or diagram (depending on the topic) in each box. Set up a 60 second visual timer (or longer if needed).

3. After the 60 seconds, learners walk around and talk to classmates, filling in any remaining boxes, front and back. Set 3–5 minutes on the timer.

4. Learners return to seats and use completed sheets for revision, essays, problem solving or as a starting point.

They then take their 'chocolate bar' for a walk around the class and ask other learners to tell them different things, filling in sections as they go. This could take three to five minutes, perhaps more if learners get into flow (and that's a great place to be!). You can gauge it in real time if learners are developing and discussing their knowledge. If some fill all eight boxes, the extension can be to go onto the back of the sheet to make up 16 boxes. Clipboards can help here too.

What is notable is that learners often know more than they realise, and the opportunity to discuss gives them a chance to reiterate. Learning is an iterative process, and you can see and hear this happening; it's very impactful. In some cases, learners start to join dots that they didn't even realise they had, and if they didn't have any, they start to get some.

For those who have no knowledge of the topic at the start, encourage them to jot down questions they may have, then their classmates can help to answer them, so everyone is included. Anyone who was initially stuck can begin to share and accumulate knowledge. The discussion draws out so much that sometimes information that had been forgotten can come back to the fore. The activity tends to run itself – clockwork, with learners spontaneously moving from person to person. You are freed up to move among the learners, ascertaining who knows what, activating and challenging, and picking up any nuggets you can use when the class comes back together.

This activity lends itself beautifully to a metacognitive follow-up. Have a pit stop and ask learners what they were:

- Realising.
- Seeing.
- Thinking.
- Noticing.
- Feeling.

You can direct this through your earlier detections. It can build resilience and get learners off first base in other situations, because they realise that if they have a go they can experience success, which is motivational.

I have seen this strategy work well in every subject across the curriculum. Symbols, emojis, formulae, annotated diagrams, predictions and pictures have all been used as successfully as words. For instance, in maths, learners could use shapes or different types of angles and their properties. In music, they could use notation, and in science, they could use chemical elements and compounds. As a subtle scaffolding technique, certain individuals could have some boxes pre-printed or have question prompts provided if helpful.

As well as using this technique at the start of a topic, it can of course be a strategy that is used to pool ideas for revision or clarification at the end, or even in the planning stages to apply to an essay or exam question, thus topping and tailing a unit of work. Another fold can also be added to crank up the challenge. Teachers are great at adapting accordingly.

Fan club

A variant of the 'walking chocolate bar' is 'fan club'. I have used this technique for launching an arguably dry topic (e.g. Elizabethan Parliaments). This is essentially another paper-folding exercise, but in this instance learners turn their piece of paper (again, coloured works well) into a fan – concertina style. I might say, 'I'm going to make you a fan of Elizabethan Parliaments' or 'We are going to be the Parliament fan club!' This is (hopefully!) energising. It helps to sell the dry topic to the class and secure learner buy-in. In this way, positivity and a can-do attitude is encouraged. It's a great one for the summer term as we all know how hot classrooms can get. It's a welcome response to 'Can we go outside?' 'Well, no, but we are making fans!' Once the fans are made (and for some you may have to quickly prepare them, or of course a study buddy can help), learners write different elements of starting-point knowledge onto the folds of the fan or ask questions. For instance, in this example, learners might write:

- 'Did Queen Elizabeth I have a prime minister?'
- 'Women definitely couldn't vote.'
- 'Was there a Labour Party?'
- 'Did Elizabeth listen to Parliament?'
- 'Did Parliament have much power?'
- 'Only rich men could make the rules, and they suited themselves.'

After logging initial information, learners then mingle with classmates and continue to write information on the folds of their fans, asking and answering questions that can then be addressed during the main body of the teaching.

Giving learners the opportunity to move around breaks up the often-sedentary nature of the day. 'Physicalising' the learning can be memorable, fun and lead to positive outcomes (Gilbert, 2025).

Cops and robbers

Taking this further, Kate Jones, in her groundbreaking debut book *Love to Teach,* suggests 'cops and robbers' as a user-friendly technique for noting down initial or retrieval information, and then 'magpieing' ideas from others to build up composite answers (Jones, 2018). A ruler can be used to divide a notebook page into a 'cops' column and a 'robbers' column. I imagine you've worked it out – learners are given four or five minutes (this timing is arbitrary and depends on starting points and intended outcomes) to jot down what they can retrieve from memory in the 'cops' column. They then have an opportunity to complete the corresponding 'robbers' column by leaving their seats and collaborating with classmates to fill in new information they have 'stolen' from each other. As with 'walking chocolate bar' and 'fan club', it is a particular joy to stand back and watch this peer interaction. Learners enjoy sharing, learning and boosting each other's knowledge. Real class camaraderie is being developed (more on this in chapter four).

Beware of underestimating young people. Often, they have cooked, played, read, sewn, created, acted, written, seen and danced before coming to you. Tap into their (often higher than you might imagine) starting points, respect them and let them demonstrate their skills and use them to propel themselves and others forwards.

3. Experts in the room

A corollary to checking starting points is finding out which of your learners are or will become the 'experts in the room'. Finding out who has a higher starting point can be helpful in terms of using these learners to help others. Badges or lanyards can be used as/if appropriate to mark a person out, and judicious use of this to ensure all feel they have a role and contribution goes without saying. How, when and if you decide to employ this strategy depends on your professional judgement based on knowledge of the class and individuals therein. In my experience, most learners respond well to this feedback and thereafter rise to the challenge of helping others. They feel they have an enhanced role to play, and it's rather like devolving another role commensurate with those in section one of this chapter.

If the idea of an 'expert' seems too boastful then launching 'learner detectives' could work. This adaptation is used at Jericho Primary School in Whitehaven, where 6-year-olds with the higher starting points have a licence (the teacher even issues imitation detective warrant cards!) to detect learning and ask questions of those who have less knowledge or understanding to clarify and deepen class-wide understanding. It is marvellous to see learners helping and encouraging each other in this way, and as with most things, the earlier this begins the more routine it becomes, and the more learners will buy in and come to expect this as the norm.

4. Study buddies

Study buddies is a catchy-sounding idea that learners tend to buy into. Soon after acquiring a new class, formally pair learners up as 'study buddies', but be very clear about what this entails. Essentially a study buddy is there to support their partner. Think of a pair of paramedics – they work in sync to get the job done. In this case, if someone is at a music lesson or a sporting practice, for instance, the study buddy can be the first port of call in terms of helping to close the gap in the case of any missing knowledge. It is incumbent upon study buddies to help each other.

You may wish to formalise this and ask learners to explicitly sign up to this role. You'll know best about what is necessary to make it binding. In *Atomic Habits*, James Clear writes of 'how an accountability partner can change everything' (Clear, 2018). Because we care about what others think about us, and we don't want them to have a lesser opinion of us, this can provide an immediate 'cost' to inaction. Beyond this, study buddies make explicit the benefits of companionship and might act as a helpful mechanism to combat anxious inaction and reduce feelings of loneliness (Gilbert, 2025). Drawing up this contract and formalising this accountability can be a useful investment of time and again, like delegation, it can be reported upon in school reports as a mark of a learner's willingness to collaborate and activate others, building those all-important interactions and relationships.

5. Home helps

It's one thing to get learners collaborating in class, but forging early links with home can be hugely beneficial in terms of supporting learner development. Patrice Bain has written extensively about the power of creating a 'teaching triangle', with the three points being learner, school and home. This is another mechanism for encouraging conversation and sociability.

One way to do this very early on is to set a homework (or preparatory research work) that involves explicit links with someone at home. This can be a sibling, carer, parent, grandparent, auntie, uncle, neighbour, whoever. Someone who can buy in to the activity and hopefully thereafter act as a reminding force for good. The work can be easy/quantifiable, and in my experience rewarding those at home with a currency universally recognised – such as gold stars – can work wonders!

For instance, I'd ask Year 7 (11-year-olds) to initially work with someone at home to draw up a list of as many Roman towns in Britain as they could. Later we would go on to spot patterns in terms of word meaning and location, but at first it was the involvement of a 'home help' and the sense of collaboration, success and satisfaction I was aiming for. The task was designed to act as a spark, a type of 'conversation kindling' for the learner and those at home. Learners had to bring the list back to class with a citation of who had helped them, plus a date and signature. I'd then look and issue the gold stickers like confetti – at least something for the learners to return home to every 'home help' who had tried, rewarding the process. I would then perhaps send a congratulatory postcard home to the top three performers in gold, silver and bronze.

A student I taught who received a postcard home, Chris Humpleby, went on to study GCSEs and A-levels and secured a place at Cambridge. At the end of his schooling when he was 18, his dad shook my hand and said, 'We still have the postcard on the fridge you sent home seven years ago when Chris and I worked together on the Roman town names.' I took that as a measure of impact; a fire had been lit!

Later in my career I joined a new local school, William Howard in Brampton, to help with A-level history teaching. I had no prior knowledge of the learners and acquired a class of 16-year-olds. I was playing catch-up and quickly trying to forge home–school relationships. I tried this 'home help' approach with these older Year 12 students. It worked equally as well; however, this time it was more complex. After a period of teaching, I set a 'teach me, tell me' task, whereby students had to go home and explain what was happening during three phases of the Vietnam War under Kennedy, Johnson and Nixon. Learners had to teach someone at home and then the 'home help' had to summarise it. Again, I got the gold stars out accordingly. Thereafter (this was a certificated class heading towards AS level in 12 months) members of the class told me that people at home would be more inclined to chase them up about their history work because we had made the gold star connection. Parents and carers had an awareness of content and expectations, and because this explicit 'sticky' memorable link had been made, history was on the busy parent/carer radar, which obviously worked in our collective favour.

6. Pass the pen

Something I see happening a lot in lessons is a teacher asking a learner to verbally explain something. The learner does their best from their seat, often with their back to the rest of the class members and their face to the teacher. This then becomes a two-way conversation between the teacher and the individual, with many other learners potentially clocking off. Sound familiar?

There is real scope here to increase the participation ratio by inviting the learner to come out to the front, pass them the pen and put them centre stage. *Some* learners may possess the skills to do this without much hesitation. However, arrange learners in pairs or threes if it helps; you know your learners best. Either way, dare to devolve and pass the pen to the learners. This way, all can see and hear.

The Oracy Skills Framework (Oracy Cambridge and Voice 21, 2018) outlines how oracy is a curricular as well as pedagogical concern, and James Mannion (one of the authors) writes that learners need to be taught how to talk: there is a significant body of knowledge that underpins the development of spoken language and communication. Fostering an understanding about oracy in ways that strengthen the educational offer is certainly worthwhile. There are many practices, routines and subject-specific curricular objectives. Clare Sealy (2024) eloquently explains why this distinction is important and why it is more helpful and realistic to say 'oracies' not 'oracy'. She puts forwards the main pedagogical reasons as being:

- Building belonging.
- Checking for understanding.
- Thinking hard.
- Using oracy to enable learners to reframe and extend their initial thoughts into a more formal speech mode (which is most directly relevant in this case).

'Pass the pen' provides an opportunity for exploratory classroom talk, a way of 'bouncing between the two' when it comes to academic language and conversational language.

The same is true when learners are given the opportunity for exploratory talk using a visualiser. I have seen primary school learners at Hensingham Primary in Whitehaven modelling maths working in this way. We could hear a pin drop as Year 1 and Year 2 classmates respectfully listened; this becomes the norm and learners know their turn will come too. Increasingly make giving learners the opportunity to speak part of your practice; it's an impactful choice. Depending on your predisposition for this, your starting point and your subject, this technique can build self-confidence, listening skills, teamwork, collaboration and cognitive development.

These benefits have been amplified in a 2024 report by the Commission on the Future of Oracy Education in England. The report says that in order to prepare young people for their future, oracy should be the fourth 'R' of education – of equal status to reading, writing and arithmetic. It calls for an increased emphasis on oracy education to better prepare all young people to become fulfilled future citizens and combat increasing polarisation and misinformation (Oracy Education Commission, 2024). So give 'pass the pen' a go and help your learners become better orators!

7. Spotlight on the students

'Pass the pen' can be taken a stage further by setting learners up in advance as 'lesson leaders'. By this I mean learners can be asked to share something or introduce a topic if they have a higher starting point. This can be a 'show and share' or they might have developed an analogy or summary technique that is helpful. They might have visited a place or have personal experience or knowledge of something from a different angle. Whatever it is, encourage creative contributions and inclusivity. Have learners 'on the stage' at the front, in pairs if that's better for your context. Either way, put the spotlight on the students.

Another way to do this is to start a lesson by putting a learner's work on display at the front as the initial focus (for example, via visualiser or iPad mirroring). As learners arrive it is very powerful to see them look for the stimulus and note that it has been generated by one of them. This arouses curiosity and reflection, and is proximal and meaningful. It is a real hook and builds a sense of expectation around who might be picked out as the star of the show. Consider making this part of your teaching routine to celebrate wonderful work. It can also be effective midway through a lesson to provide inspiration, reinforcing expectations and celebrating excellence and/or effort.

There might be scope to swap about with your colleagues too. You can share scripts or make guest appearances in each other's lessons. We often had departmental members undertaking 'hot seat' activities, where they sat centrally as a historic character and learners asked them questions. Mrs Paterson with her Glaswegian accent would be Mary, Queen of Scots. She'd blow the learners' minds by telling them that although Mary was born at Linlithgow Palace, she would have spoken French and had a French accent as her father died when she was six days old. She inherited the throne, and she was brought up in France while Scotland was governed by regents. As you can imagine this approach was different, memorable and generated lots of learners' questions.

Using an audio recording can add another scholarly dimension too: readings, explainer videos and podcasts all add a different voice and attract attention. Even asking a colleague to make an audio recording or a guest speaker to contribute can have impact. Think about who else can be the voice of authority so messages are further reinforced.

8. Flo's feedback

As a history department we shuffled the curriculum running order in terms of how the subject offering should be cumulatively shaped, building backwards from the final expected outcomes. We tried to keep up to date with current scholarship and used enquiry questions – the cornerstone of history teaching – to direct the learning (Keates, Stanford and Goullée, 2025). We were always tweaking lessons to fit in with sensible timescales around options, assessments and fieldwork, and we increasingly aligned with the idea of *Teaching Backwards*: 'a thinking process that enables teachers to plan and teach backwards from a clear and well-defined destination' (Griffith and Burns, 2014).

Learner subject buy-in is vital for option choice numbers and the size, strength and importance of the department, and ultimately to secure teaching jobs. As well as the subject expertise and rigour, we liked to pride ourselves on always looking for novel ways to enthuse and excite our learners. A rather unconventional approach I used that really built learner interest goes as follows...

The history corridor was famously served by lovely, long-serving cleaner, Flo, who was a real hit with the students. At the end of every school day, learners would be leaving and Flo would be ready to come into the classroom with her cloth, bucket and Henry hoover! Along with Joyce and Noeleen, Flo had her break in my room around 4.45pm, and that's when the real business of the day was done. What they didn't know about the students wasn't worth knowing. They were around the building all day. They encountered students on arrival, in the lunch queue and in the corridors, and had over 90 years' experience between them, so they knew all the families in the community.

One day I had a class eager for a quick response to their efforts, so I decided to use 'Flo's feedback' as a novel cheerleading approach to recognise work done well. I asked Flo to literally cast a glance over the open exercise books on the desks. I asked her to pick a first, second and third, she told me her rationale and I made a note. She made some helpful general comments too. The learners loved it! It wasn't forensic feedback by any means; it was just the idea that there was an audience – that someone else was looking.

Over time I tailored what I was looking for to what Flo was looking for, and the 'audience effect' certainly made a difference. I got three rosettes – gold, silver and bronze. I issued them to Flo and asked her to mix up the awarding of rosettes and noticed progress. The learners may well have been influenced by the Hawthorne effect, which refers to a tendency by some individuals to alter their behaviour in response to their awareness of being observed. I was aware of the novelty value of this and that the effect may well wear off (Perera, 2024), so it wasn't something I continually used, but it became part of the feedback armoury linked to habits and learner motivation.

Learners really appreciated this, and it certainly helped increase expectations and improve outcomes. More casually, members of the history department used to pop in and out of each other's classes in an inquisitive, cheerleading kind of way. For instance, I might prime a class and say, 'Mrs Paterson, Mrs Barnsley, Mrs Heywood, Mr Hurst, Mr Bloy or Mr Dalton might be popping in. They are interested to hear your thoughts on Robert Owen, so be ready to give them your views if they ask you.' This didn't undermine anyone's credibility; that is very important. We knew each other and the learners enough to know this visitation would have an elevating effect. You might pick a pilot class to try something like this with or think how an audience effect could work in your setting.

9. Prop it up

Props can really embolden learners and add gravitas to the proceedings. For instance, microphones, clipboards, lanyards, badges, lab coats, chef hats, palettes and toolboxes can literally, for some learners, be something to hang on to, which helps build confidence. They serve to add an air of authority and bolster learners' willingness to present, explain and instruct others. Props help learners take on a role – the mantle of the expert, perhaps. I'm not necessarily suggesting we all don capes and play at superheroes, although interestingly the Latin word for cape, *cappa*, forms the basis for the word 'escape', which comes from *ex cappa*. 'To *escape*,' wrote Walter William Skeat in *An Etymological Dictionary of the English Language*, 'is to *ex-cape* oneself, to slip out of one's cape and get away' (Morton, 2015). Learners tell me they feel more inclined and 'in role' if supported by a prop.

Practical props in my experience are memorable and help to maximise learning, but we must always be mindful of avoiding the split attention effect. 'Most of the time, the split attention effect is experienced with multimedia' (Harvard, 2025). This effect occurs when learners have to divide their attention between two sources of information that have been split either temporally or spatially. The props I am suggesting are intrinsic, chosen carefully to support focus and engagement without creating extra cognitive load.

Mini-whiteboards (MWBs) are clearly more than a prop. They are an integral part of many lessons, helping to include everyone and increase the participation ratio. How to implement and optimise the use of these unsung heroes of the classroom has been well documented, most recently in Jamie Clark's excellent *Teaching One-Pagers* (Clark, 2024). He includes guidance on how to establish routines and capture precise data. In the maths department at Mearns Castle in East Renfrewshire they have run with the MWBs by purchasing the biggest available. Learners have responded very well to these, automatically dividing the MWBs in half so there is room to show both the answer **and** the working out. The teachers pick out boards to show and share, and sometimes place them under a visualiser to give live feedback. On occasion, there is scope to show and spin the MWBs so that learners can see each other's. In this way they can refine classmate contributions, celebrate success, and unpick errors and misconceptions. Again, judicious use of this is needed, but it can help to build class camaraderie. It is rarely done and arguably a trick is missed in that the teacher is the only one seeing the boards, and learners just see each other's heads. Try to take a 360° immersive view of your classroom whenever possible.

For schools with digital devices, Whiteboard.fi is a fabulous digital MWB solution, which the MFL department at Portobello High School, Edinburgh use to great effect. In this instance, learners' individual responses all appear on the screen at the front of the class, thus making thinking visible. All can see and discuss each other's answers, detecting success and correcting errors to close gaps.

Digital developments are ongoing, and I've seen some cutting edge technology with the functionality of Magma Maths at St Thomas Aquinas in Glasgow. Beyond the 'send to all', teachers can see, track and analyse how many attempts a learner took to solve a problem. A composite record of whole-class success also racks up as a visible running tally, and this seems to motivate everyone as they continue to play their part (however big or small the contribution) and enjoy the fanfare when a milestone is reached (which can be customised and set by the teacher). This encourages class camaraderie and a sense of community, the focus of chapter four.

10. Avoid repetition

Test yourself – how many times when a learner answers a question do you automatically repeat their answer? Just consciously check and see (or ask a second pair of eyes to look). Chances are you do it **a lot**; most people do.

This is a huge finding when observing lessons. The majority (anecdotally, I'd say 90%) of teachers do it automatically and sometimes without being aware; it is an unconscious habit. Sometimes it may be the right thing to do if it truly is something that needs emphasis and perhaps exemplification. In the main, however, it can really slow the pace of the lesson, and often the teacher modifies a learner's answer to be what suits them rather than what the learner has said.

This can be a little disheartening or disempowering for the learner who volunteered their best effort. I have learned this through student voice work. If you feel something needs amplification, ask the learner to repeat it. If you repeat it constantly, there is the danger that the learners don't listen to each other. They tune out because they know you will reiterate or even change it. Not listening to each other can prevent a lot of learning. Listening is important and often underrated (see chapter one, section nine for more). If peer-to-peer listening is not actively encouraged, there is the risk of learners switching off and becoming reliant upon you. This is something to avoid since you are hopefully aiming to develop knowledgeable, independent learners who are increasingly self-regulating.

Bear in mind: if learners have hearing difficulties, hopefully they will have hearing aids. You might have a transmitter (as I did for a wonderful A-level student of mine) or have their seating position optimised for lip reading.

11. Activating and challenging

If you are daring to devolve in the ways described above, where do you fit in? What's your part in all this? The benefits are huge. You are freed up to walk around the room to activate and challenge learners, ask probing questions and give real-time effective feedback that is task-specific, subject-specific or linked to self-regulation.

Thinking about your classroom positioning is also important for a clockwork classroom. If you were to create a heat map of your movements, where would you be? Do you wear a hole in the carpet at the front of the room, or are you confined behind a monitor? On both counts, learners may well go under the radar. Are you going right to left at the front? Do you not routinely make it around the sides or to the back of the room? Perhaps those learners who are further away could potentially disengage? For them it might be a case of 'quick, look busy, they're coming' when you make a rare visit, whereas if you make your presence a norm, disengagement can be prevented. A teacher at Glenrothes High School in Fife recently told me that getting around the room had been a game changer for her to get to know learners and develop relationships. This is certainly something you could track, or a trusted second pair of eyes could help you use the 'have a go' template at the back of the book.

If you have dared to devolve in the ways suggested, you can thank me later when you experience your learners doing more of the heavy lifting to everyone's benefit.

Takeaways – think very carefully about how and when you can devolve to your learners

- Issue jobs and emphasise being purposeful.
- Routinely check starting points for knowledge and understanding, and remedy any misconceptions.
- Detect who has a high starting point and utilise them as appropriate.
- Match learners up in supportive pairs – make that the norm.
- Sometimes devise tasks that will involve teaming up with trusted family, friends or caregivers.
- Make showing and telling at the front by learners part of the usual repertoire.
- Spotlight on the students whenever possible, allowing them and their work to shine.
- Involve an external audience or interested party whenever appropriate.

- Use props to the best advantage in your setting.
- Avoid repeating learners' answers and ask them to repeat if necessary.
- Walk around and work the room.

Now it's your turn

- Use the template on page 102 to have a go at some of the 11 strategies that underpin the principles of 'dare to devolve'.
- Remember to persevere to make it routine.
- Set yourself one or more intentions and pledge to review your ongoing progress.

Recommended reading

- *Love to Teach* – Kate Jones.
- *Talk-Less Teaching* – Isabella Wallace and Leah Kirkham.

Chapter 4 map

Class camaraderie and a sense of community

1		Make it personal
2		Secret spies
3		KASH converters
4		On patrol
5		Lesson of luxury
6		Best seat in the house
7		Going golden
8		Consensus – casseroling the conversation
9		Plan for 'collective effervescence'
10		Metacognition

Chapter 4:
Class camaraderie and a sense of community

'Friendship is the hardest thing in the world to explain ... if you haven't learned the meaning of friendship, you haven't really learned anything.' Muhammad Ali, 1962

'The most important factor in making people happy in their work is a sense of belonging' (Camilleri, 2024). To this end, schools have all kinds of inclusive values and mottos, but the danger is they are platitudes – just for show. Ideas need to be lived, not laminated, as often discussed by Mary Myatt (2023). One school that really does live the strapline is Rainford High, St Helens: 'Everyone counts, everyone helps, everyone succeeds' or *todos cuentan, todos ayudan, todos triunfan* in Spanish (it is displayed in multiple languages). This emphasis on 'everyone' and the connectivity of the moving parts develops collegiality. So, endeavour to make it 'our' classroom as much as you can. A shared space and experience where everyone is valued and encouraged to contribute in 'our' lesson. A consensual ethos where everyone matters. Engender a sense of 'us' to develop and harness classroom camaraderie.

So, how to live it? Much is written about how to get adults to successfully work together. In his book *The Power of Teams*, Sam Crome (2023) writes, 'There is no perfect formula.' He makes recommendations for creating a team whose members push each other to reach their potential, discuss freely, foresee issues, adapt to what's going on and commit to the team's work. I like the phrase he uses: members are 'journeying with you'. Crome outlines the need for belonging, values, shared vision, roles, goals, communication, dynamism, and a domain-specific remit and body of knowledge. So, how could this apply to learners? Of course, you receive a class of individuals who have different starting points. You are ambitious for them, and they are hopefully ambitious for themselves, but what if they were ambitious for each other? What if they became invested in the team's development and improvement? As the popular phrase goes, 'A rising tide lifts all boats.' They are journeying together through their school days. How might this translate into productive work and a culture of learning and growth as a group? It all sounds great in theory, but how to do it in practice? Given the overwhelming evidence for the benefits of being part of a group, this chapter suggests some ways to harness classroom peer power.

When former Liverpool FC manager Jürgen Klopp was the manager of Borussia Dortmund, he made it clear to executives at the club that they had to develop this feeling of 'we' in an attempt to build collective strength. Sarina Wiegman DBE – the Lionesses' head coach who led them to historic victory in the UEFA Final July 2025 – said, 'The bonding in this team has been incredible. I think that gave us the edge – I think we were the best bonded team' (Hunt, 2025).

In recent times we have sadly been made acutely aware of the need for community; the importance of human connection and collective strength when we were cut off from each other due to the Covid-19 pandemic. We should encourage young people to take away any learning they can to propel them forwards into making positive choices as adults. Our backgrounds and experiences often shape our futures. Growing up as a teenager in Whitehaven in geographically isolated West Cumbria during the 1980s at the time of the Miner's Strike, 'coal not dole' was the mantra. Many of my friend's fathers were miners, and we made food parcels and pitched in. On reflection, perhaps our teachers at St Benedict's RC high school during these difficult times thought how best to develop our sense of camaraderie and community. It never occurred to me then, but there were little touches that seemed to be ahead of the times. Our form tutor, Mrs Haig, issued us all with engraved pens with 'Haig's Super Group' etched on, and instantly we were bonded together by this. Aged 13, we thought we were invincible. She was like a lioness looking after us, and we thrived on it! I believe I subconsciously tried to replicate her approach when I first became a form tutor almost 10 years later. In a way, Mrs Haig was amplifying a collectivist culture, something Owen Eastwood explores in his book *Belonging* (Eastwood, 2022). He draws upon his heritage to centralise the Māori idea of *whakapapa,* which embodies our universal need to belong. He places this concept at the core of his methods, an ethos that has made him one of the most in-demand performance coaches in the world.

In my role as head of department, I was responsible for GCSE and A-level results and constantly thinking about every possible action or intervention we could take in class time and beyond to enhance outcomes for learners. What worked? What didn't? Why not? How could we explain it? This came sharply into focus annually at number-crunch time after exam results. I noticed on a five-year cycle, when the history department were the form tutors for six Year 11 forms, the results saw an upsurge. I can only attribute this to the fact that we built teams and kept close tabs on our final year students, cheerleading them morning and afternoon in registration time, reiterating what needed to be done. This habitual proximity and consistency, pinpointing individuals and small groups (leading by numbers), helped build routines and reminders that led to this success. It further reinforced my anecdotal research about rigour and accountability.

Learners were also invited to CPD sessions and evaluation opportunities, which gave us a chance to unpick the pros and cons of approaches we had used or were about to use from their learner perspective. They stayed behind after school for twilight sessions and made some insightful points. We tended to ensure their time was rewarded with tea, cakes, vouchers and of course a mention in dispatches immediately and in later school reports.

These were embryonic 'slice teams' as popularised by Dr James Mannion – a key part of implementation science where a cross-section of the school community sits around the decision-making table together. A preferable alternative to a top-down approach in terms of making change stick (Mannion, 2025).

While these teams are temporary for the duration of school life, we all know lifelong friendships can be made with individual classmates and colleagues. I have been lucky enough to have enjoyed both. 'In spirit, the best teams last for ever' (Sinfield, 2023).

1. Make it personal

A neat way of reinforcing a sense of 'us' is by finding every opportunity in your planning and delivery to showcase the work of classroom-based learners and using their names. For instance, as the class arrives, hook them in by displaying some of their work under the visualiser. Immediately they will be discussing, 'Is that yours?' 'Whose is that?' The sense of collegiality will be amplified. When offering any direct instruction, analogies, stories or examples, endeavour to explicitly use learners' names as appropriate, and mix it up to be as inclusive as possible. This helps to make the lesson content memorable and fosters a sense of belonging and care.

2. Secret spies

This is a genius idea from Isabella Wallace and Leah Kirkham (2014), which has been used and adapted with great success across a range of settings. Essentially, the teacher uses learners to 'spy' on each other to catch their classmates doing well.

How the spy is assigned is open to teacher preference. I initially met the learners at the door with a tub of counters. They each took one on arrival. It was either a blank counter or had an 's' to denote 'spy' marked on. I tended to have three spies in a class of 30 initially, to front-load the idea, and then I reduced the number to two or one as the class developed the understanding that they all needed to habitually work together to succeed.

Other teachers have other identification methods. One English teacher I work with always hides a Post-it note on the requisite page of a novel, play, poem anthology or textbook, and the spy finds it when they start to read. The class know to surreptitiously open their books – slick! Hazel Taylor in the MFL department at Portobello High School, Edinburgh emails the spy in advance so no mention needs to be made in class until the reveal at the end of the session – clockwork! Teachers are brilliantly creative, so think about what might work best for you.

Once the spy is in place it is their responsibility to listen, keep a look out, and at the end of the lesson, day, week or topic (again, you decide!), they reveal themselves and outline who they caught doing well and why. I found short-term gratification works best by rounding off lessons with the spies revealing themselves and talking us through the lesson highlights. A spy's reasons for who they selected can be totally open-ended – interesting questions, valid contributions, effort, attainment, impressive progress, teamworking – whatever the spy decides. In a culture of high expectations and excellence, valid reasons are given.

3. KASH converters

In this technique, learners are given the task of spotting good KASH – knowledge, attitudes, skills and habits. This needn't be done covertly; in fact, I have seen it used to great effect in many PE departments whereby those who are not actively participating are the observers, and they have the job of picking out performance highlights to emphasise or highlight at the end of the session. This is based on the work of Griffith and Burns (2014).

The reveal ending in all cases is so impactful – a lovely, positive finale to a lesson. Those involved (which will be pretty much everyone over a period of time) can be named in report writing, positive phone calls home and parents' evenings.

Learners often share with others at home that they were the KASH convertor, for instance, or that they were spied upon, and that further strengthens the 'teaching triangle' (see chapter three, section five) of learner, parents/carers and school. I like to think these strategies will help you pass the 'tea-time test' when it is your lesson that is being talked about in homes across the catchment area during evening mealtime!

4. On patrol

Rather like 'experts in the room' (chapter three, section three), in this case selected learners can go 'on patrol' in the classroom, checking on something specific that you have assigned to them.

Clearly, trust needs to be built here, and the earlier this is made a norm, the more likely learners are to embrace it and genuinely get involved (this is often easier with younger learners). The classic example taken from Kate Jones (2018) involves learners going on 'SPaG watch'. In this case they get a high-vis jacket and check on spelling, punctuation and grammar. Depending on the age and stage of your learners, you may wish to break it down further to 'spelling squad' or 'punctuation police'. At one school I work in, the teachers decided to create SPaG wristbands, because the wearing of a wristband was associated with entry to a gig or festival, which appealed to learners. Whatever method you use to help learners run the rule over their peers can be made into a patrol. At Lochgelly High School in Fife, Scotland, Mr Argo assigned 'Argo's accuracies'. These individuals in the business and enterprise department checked over classmates' work paying extra attention to detail to help strive for excellence.

5. Lesson of luxury

I visited Rainford High to film a newly qualified teacher. As the
class were lined up outside the room, they were asking each other,
'Who do you think has got the cushion?' Intrigued, I entered the classroom
with them. They took their seats and waited, silently, expectantly, for the
big reveal. Their teacher revealed that she had awarded the 'cushion of
comfort' to Ciara for her thought-provoking question the day before. This
meant that Ciara would be awarded a cushion of comfort to enjoy the
lesson of luxury. I was astounded by how well the class took to this, and
the members were 16 or 17 years old! The cushion was a coveted item,
and it really helped build class camaraderie and ensure learners had high
expectations of themselves and each other.

A variation was that learners could vote on a slip placed in a box at the end
of the lesson for who they thought should receive the cushion next time,
and of course there was a trusted vote counter so as not to make any extra
work for the teacher.

I have seen this idea used to great effect in many schools. An amp-shaped musical cushion was used in the music department at Bell Baxter High School in Fife, Scotland – when a button was pushed, a guitar riff played. A fabric number maths cushion was used at Hilbre High School on the Wirral, a sequin-covered cushion in the MFL department at Whitehaven Academy and religious icon cross-stich cushions were used at St Thomas Aquinas, Glasgow. Choose something that best suits your classroom.

6. Best seat in the house

This is rather like 'lesson of luxury' but instead of a cushion, there is a dedicated chair. Some teachers I work with offer their own chair temporarily to a learner. It's called 'the chair of champions' by Mhairi Sneddon and the science department at St Mungo's School in Glasgow. Others have a different fancy chair in class or a way of adorning a mobility chair or walking aid. At Bransty Primary School there are two old chairs that have been upcycled with decoupage superhero deigns. Learners covet the chance to be awarded the privilege to use them as their seats. For younger learners, a special carpet square to sit on is awarded to an individual in the Year 1 class at Yewdale Primary School, Carlisle who has made an impressive contribution to the learning of the group.

7. Going golden

Another talking point that really helps to develop a sense of belonging, community and camaraderie is 'going golden'. I have seen this successfully used across multiple schools and departments. The premise is that extra kudos is given to an individual or group who make a standout contribution, and they have the honour of using some golden equipment. This might be the golden Bunsen burner (spraypainted of course!) as at Trinity School, Carlisle, or the golden toolkit in the DET (design and engineering technology) department at Lochgelly High School. The science department at Portobello uses golden goggles. Wooden spoon, toolbox, paint brush, calculator, drumsticks – you name it! These pieces of equipment can be awarded alongside certificates, such as the one pictured here. Think about how you can include this technique in your repertoire.

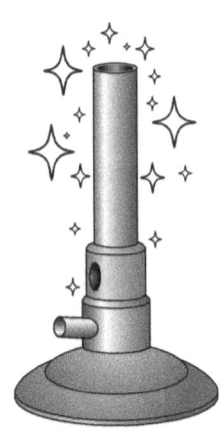

Bunsen burner licence

This certifies that Kaitlin has demonstrated the ability to:

- Identify and name the parts of a Bunsen burner
- Set up a Bunsen burner correctly and light it safely
- Adjust the flame appropriately and use the Bunsen burner safely

The holder of this licence may therefore use a Bunsen burner in the lab if directed to do so by a teacher.

Signed: Mr Sullivan   Date: September 2025

8. Consensus – casseroling the conversation

It is an instructional illusion (Kirschner, Hendrick and Heal, 2025) that faster learning is better. Deep, meaningful learning requires time, refinement, rumination, rehearsal and the application of mental effort. Sharing experiences, compromise and discussion is a huge part of being in school, and slowing the pace can help forge new connections, developing a sense of camaraderie and community. A practical classroom-based way to do this is by encouraging learners to reach consensus.

My esteemed Historical Association (HA) colleague Diana Laffin coined the exquisite phrase 'casseroling the conversation', and a consensus activity allows scope for that – a rare opportunity in classrooms to slow things down in an environment that is often rushed. The activity encourages learners to take stock, guide each other, regulate themselves and think carefully about where to place emphasis. According to a Demos report that polled 700 16–18-year-olds, 'schools are closing down space for debate and discussion' (Gamote and Hyman, 2025) leaving learners craving honest discussion, which suggests this activity may be well received.

Learners are given a large sheet of paper with a question (or a statement, translation, numerical problem, illustration – whatever it might be) placed in the middle. Learners respond to it individually first, and then collectively. They may have to provide an answer, solution, corrections, annotations or translation – you decide. The individuals can work in groups of four, each taking a quadrant of the paper to write their initial individual thoughts down to meet the challenge set. This approach ensures each learner is accountable for their quarter of the paper, avoids passengers (those learners lettings others do the work) and cranks up the participation ratio. Once individuals have had time to think and jot down their thoughts, it's time to share and reach a composite response – consensus.

It might be wise to bring in this opportunity to provide a shared experience and slow the pace on occasion. I have seen learners very absorbed in this activity when trying to formulate an exam answer, refining their thoughts towards the end of the academic year or in the run-up to formal assessment, for instance.

If the idea of debating and exploring appeals, the Historical Association's Secondary Committee (2025) have recently issued a set of cards – 'Driving your discussion' – which might provide you with the opportunity to take part in some professional departmental casseroling!

9. Plan for 'collective effervescence'

Think explicitly about how you might develop collective identity, seek out ways to engage the class and make them feel part of something bigger. The great pioneering social scientist Émile Durkheim coined the term 'collective effervescence' to describe the sense of energy and power that people experience when they come together for a shared purpose (Daisley, 2023).

The idea of effervescence naturally reminds me of my chemistry teacher at St Benedict's, Mr Cox. He was a subject expert who recognised the bonding (no pun intended) power of camaraderie and importance of social interconnectedness. He knew that the fizzing due to the release of carbon dioxide when adding hydrochloric acid to calcium carbonate was something his class would marvel at. His favourite feigned surprise exclamation was 'Jumping Jack Flash, it's a gas, gas, gas!' He'd smile and say with his twinkly eyes and reassuring Lancashire accent: 'One more time for the kiddies?!' Then repeat the experiment. We were 16 and we loved it! He captured our collective imagination. It was a tried-and-tested 'Eureka!' moment. I was about 25 before I realised he was quoting Rolling Stones lyrics, but that didn't matter. He made the learning 'sticky', memorable and we had all become part of something bigger.

In teaching, a sure-fire strategy that many teachers naturally adopt is a **pre**-mortem. Mr Cox always did this. He knew where the 'magic moments' lay within his curriculum, and he aimed to allow us the time to savour them. Clearly, we can't legislate for everything. There are so many variables when dealing with human beings and most are beyond our control, but before you do anything, think through all the possible permutations: 'If I do X, Y might happen. If I do Y, Z might happen.' And so on. Aim to close any gaps before they appear. A **post**-mortem is too little, too late. Think carefully about how best to maximise learner participation. To think everything through clearly, it is important to have your intended outcome at the forefront of your thoughts.

10. Metacognition

Metacognition is classically defined as knowing about knowing. Metacognitive ability is thus a critical capacity in human beings, linked to our ability to learn, make good decisions, interact with others and know ourselves (Rahnev, 2025). Eric Sotto in his book *When Teaching Becomes Learning* says, 'I have managed to suggest two things: one, that learning is to a considerable extent a matter of being open to the world. And two, that answers must be found inside one's own head' (Sotto, 2007).

It might seem counterintuitive in a chapter about class camaraderie and developing a sense of community to be proposing a focus on sharing what is 'inside one's own head', but metacognition contributes to educational efficiency at the individual, classroom and institutional levels (Ishak, Oderinde and Ahmad, 2025). Beyond the immediate academic benefits, developing metacognitive strategies also holds the potential to promote lifelong learning skills and that is of paramount importance.

So, how to do it? Routinely being open about how you, as a teacher, plan, approach and remember things (however silly!) can pay dividends. 'Modelling by the teacher is a cornerstone of effective teaching; revealing the thought processes of an expert learner helps to develop pupils' metacognitive skills' (EEF, 2025). Regularly asking learners 'How will you remember this?' encourages them to share anecdotes, analogies, mnemonics, metaphors, stories and other associations that help them to develop the mental connections and commit information to memory. This focus on metacognition, an awareness of one's thought processes and an understanding of the patterns behind them has been found to be very impactful. The Sutton Trust-EEF Teaching and Learning Toolkit –

which summarises international evidence – rates metacognition and self-regulation as a high-impact, low-cost approach to improving the attainment of disadvantaged learners.

Studies have reported 'a substantial average effect size of 0.808 in learning outcomes when metacognitive strategies are systematically implemented, highlighting their transformative potential in education' (Ishak, Oderinde and Ahmad, 2025). Findings showed learners become more efficient at meeting challenges through strategising and systematically applying useful metacognitive approaches. This strengthens autonomy and independence, and leads to improved time management – clockwork!

In Stem subjects an emphasis on metacognition increased problem-solving accuracy, while in humanities subjects it supported reflective practices such as critical reading and writing (ibid., 2025).

While metacognition is essentially a personal pursuit, explicitly planning exploratory opportunities to place emphasis upon this and build it into your teaching mean learners pick up on it as a useful technique. They may adopt the approach if it's made routine and start to 'have a word' with themselves when approaching tasks and committing information to memory. I've had some classroom success in this regard by periodically building in a 'pit stop' and asking learners to be reflexive putting their mind to the following stems:

- I'm thinking…
- I'm noticing…
- I'm wondering…
- I'm seeing…
- I'm feeling…
- I'm realising…

This openness means learners often find common ground; an educational affinity. It can help to forge relationships. It's a low-stakes exercise since a learner can't be 'wrong' about what was in their head. Allowing a bit of time for paired, table and whole-class talk can uncover common preconceptions, misconceptions and collective ways forwards, which can often be revelatory, fun and help expedite the learning process.

The 'walking chocolate bar' activity in chapter three lends itself beautifully to a metacognitive follow-up. It can build resilience and get learners off first base in other situations, since they realise that if they have a go, they can experience success. I think it was most pithily put by Hattie and Yates: 'Learning is optimised when teachers see learning through the eyes of the learner, and when learners see themselves as their own teachers' (Hattie and Yates, 2013).

Takeaways – develop belonging and togetherness

- Reinforce a sense of 'us'.
- Allocate learners to be 'secret spies', thus sharing lesson highlights and building class camaraderie.
- Involve all in converting habits and spotting good ones.
- Use learners to go 'on patrol', identifying excellence and improvements.
- Ensure learners understand impressive classroom contributions.
- Celebrate stand-out moments with coveted visible privileges.
- Ensure learners aim high and strive to be 'the golden ones'.
- Slow down and allow deliberate time for talk.
- Ensure pre-mortems plan backwards from potential 'eureka' moments.
- Build in time for learners to have a word with themselves – metacognition – and share the thinking.

Now it's your turn

- Use the template on page 102 to have a go at some of the 10 strategies that underpin the principle of 'class camaraderie and building a sense of community'.
- Remember to persevere in order to make it routine.
- Set yourself one or more intentions and pledge to review your ongoing progress.

Recommended reading

- *The Power of Teams* – Sam Crome.
- *Fortitude* – Bruce Daisley.
- *Belonging* – Owen Eastwood.

Chapter 5 map

Classroom connoisseurs

1		Quality features checklist
2		Show and tell
3		Find and fix
4		Peer marking agreement
5		Frame it and tame it
6		Ready for a receipt?
7		Genius bank
8		Work selfies
9		Super scholars
10		Learning detectives

Chapter 5:
Classroom connoisseurs

'Be a yardstick of quality. Some people aren't used to an environment where excellence is expected.' Steve Jobs

When we go to a fancy restaurant, we usually know what quality looks like. The same is true of an art gallery, a car showroom or a clothes boutique – we have in our mind's eye an understanding. This chapter is about equipping learners with the insider knowledge they need in order to know excellence when they see it, hear it, taste it and read it.

Exposure to quality and excellence is vital so that learners have that rich understanding of the options and possibilities. During my time at St Aidan's, a mixed 11–18 comprehensive school in north Cumbria, we were constantly taking learners on cultural experiences to castles, museums, historic houses, archives and theatres, and inviting in performers, musicians and guest speakers. We also signed up to whole-class online sessions so learners could broaden their horizons, opening up their worlds to new and exciting creative possibilities. We looked to 'provide innovative practice, locally tailored content, and enrichment activities that help ensure young people thrive in education and later life' (Francis, 2025). Good to know we were in line with recommended practice around enrichment opportunities!

Sometimes it took a bit of nudging to get learners involved, and imposter syndrome was clear on occasion. The intention behind offering these opportunities was to encourage young people to 'roll up your sleeves and take the world by storm' (Mosse, 2025), to make them aware that they were global citizens and ultimately to work towards bridging the gap between novice and expert.

Being ambitious in class is a good starting point for crafting classroom connoisseurs by developing an ethic of excellence. Aiming high and sharing scholarship with learners can yield fruitful results. Avoid underestimating learners – their starting points are often higher than you think.

Educators should beware the 'curse of knowledge'. This phrase was coined in 1989 by economists Camerer, Loewenstein and Weber (Jones, 2023) and it refers to a cognitive bias where individuals assume other people know what they know, and we simply can't remember what it was like not to know. Sometimes called the 'empathy gap', it can provide a frustrating barrier to effective teaching because we can't recreate our learners' state of mind and starting points. For Christine Counsell, the curse being 'that we, policy makers and leaders, simply forget what journeys gave us the accomplished fluency we now have – whether acquired through our own systematic education or through the privileges of cultural advantage in our youth or childhood, or both' (Counsell, 2025).

Consider using specialists in your field to inspire and captivate your learners, whether that be through video demonstrations, audio recordings, podcasts, 'live lessons' (for example, lessons from the BBC or the National Archives), journals, articles, stories or books. Include scholarship to bring that richness to lessons. I saw footage of the synchronised swimming and gymnastics at the 2024 Paris Olympics used to great effect by Erin Green with National 5 PE students at Glenrothes High School in Fife. Learners were rapt, in awe of what is possible. In my classroom experience, exposure to excellence doesn't serve to demoralise but to inspire; to encourage learners to ask questions, wonder and strive.

Subject associations can often help here, and universities sometimes have outreach budgets, which means academic experts can link up with schools. For instance, Dr Sarah Longair and Sasha Smith have recently collaborated on an 'Objects of Empire' venture in Lincolnshire, which is a fascinating way into learning about the British Empire through using material culture (Bones, Smith and Longair, 2025). Through handling artefacts and hearing from experts, lessons are elevated and possibilities explored.

You may have heard of the mnemonic WAGOLL – what a good one looks like (or sounds, feels or tastes like, depending on your subject). This idea may sound gimmicky, but at its heart is the need to emphasise the importance of high-quality work and high expectations. The use of a partly formed 'good one' for scaffolding through modelling is explored by Rachel Ball and Alex Fairlamb (2025) in chapter three of their book *The*

Scaffolding Effect. In this way, learners can see what a *developing* product looks like. The benefits of exposing learners to excellence has been popularised by Ron Berger in his book *An Ethic of Excellence* (Berger, 2003). Capture and collect great work created by your learners and keep it to hand for other learners to see. Call some students' completed exam scripts back from the exam board. Have a bank of WAGOLL examples to refer to. If you gather work at various levels and stages, this can help learners see and understand the differences.

This approach is useful for staff development and moderation too. When I was a head of department, to ensure consistency and a readiness to apply the rubric with new colleagues, we often went through some sample scripts together. Showing as well as telling is great for exemplification and learner understanding. The opportunity to look or listen again and unpick a piece of work is something learners and teachers have repeatedly told me they find beneficial. Learning is a reiterative process, so continued exposure to excellence encourages everybody involved to aim high.

How can we practically develop and encourage connoisseurship in the classroom?

1. Quality features checklist

Firstly, familiarise your learners with something top-notch from your subject and go through it with them, analysing what makes it so good. As a collective, you will be able to co-create success criteria. As with most things, be sure to pre-mortem this yourself, know the ingredients that have led to the quality item and provide learners with the opportunity to identify them. You might choose to do this as a whole class, in pairs or alone. You might take a graduated 'I do, we do, you do' approach, which begins with you explaining or demonstrating alone, followed by supporting your learners to do the same thing, and finally releasing responsibility fully to learners. It's best to allow some scope for discussion. As with most things, it depends upon the starting points of your learners as to how much scaffolding might be needed.

Have the item close to the learners, and ensure they jot down their ideas on a mini-whiteboard, book or even on the desk or table so they can refine their thoughts and then wipe it away. I have found permitting learners to 'go large' and write on their actual desks has been novel and motivational, provided non-permanent pens are in use of course! Ask your learners specifically **why** the example is so good, and draw up a 'quality features checklist' together. Learners can often be more discerning than we initially give them credit for. In my work filming teachers in action, teachers sometimes see that they have underestimated what their learners can do and realise that next time, they should crank up the challenge earlier. Drawing up a list isn't exhaustive and clearly doesn't necessarily mean that learners can replicate the level of quality, but they at least have a blueprint that they can work towards. It's no longer an unknown challenge. The depth and range of what is expected of course depends on the starting point and context; this is where your professional judgement comes in. The expectation is that equipped with the 'quality features checklist' learners will go on to hold themselves and each other to account, thus leading to increased self-regulation, automaticity and less reliance on you – clockwork.

Developing these metacognitive processes habitually with an accompanying insistence on high standards provides preparation for future learning and helps to make inroads when it comes to the transfer illusion. 'The transfer illusion reveals a fundamental tension in educational design: the conditions that optimise immediate performance often differ dramatically from those that enable long-term application across diverse contexts' (Kirschner, Hendrick and Heal, 2025).

A way to scaffold this further is to use worked examples. Worked examples are a pre-solved problem or completed task with step-by-step stages to success thoroughly explained. It's rather like using a recipe for the first time. Perhaps you can relate to how this might be followed slavishly the first time you cook a particular dish, then reliance upon the recipe fades over time with more practice. In *The Scaffolding Effect,* Rachel Ball and Alex Fairlamb (2025) share Bob Pritchard's FAME suggestion for the retraction of worked examples and a progression in instructional design:

- **Fading**: Fading away steps in a process after providing fully worked examples to maintain challenge.

- **Alternating**: Alternating worked examples with opportunities for students to try a similar independent example.

- **Mistakes**: Include mistakes in worked examples so students can apply their knowledge to deepen understanding.

- **Explanation**: Teachers can use a think-aloud process to help students make sense of the model.

2. Show and tell

Lessons can involve a lot of listening. That is a fact, and it's no bad thing. However, sometimes a more efficient and effective way of working is to **show** learners what you mean. This happens routinely in some parts of the school; demonstrations in science, PE, home economics, design and technology – see the 'gather and go' approach as outlined in chapter one. Similarly in art and music lessons, learners gathering to see the work is often the norm, enhanced by overhead projectors, visualisers or iPads. At St Thomas Aquinas high school in Glasgow, Principal Teacher Loraine Tierney made how-to films to illustrate techniques in art. These films unobtrusively played in the background in class on a loop so the learners could refer to them while they were in the flow of being creative. This freed Loraine up to help individuals, and it develops learners' self-regulation skills. This is the 'I do, we do, you do' continuum in action. There is far more scope for this across the curriculum. Many young people are now naturally used to finding hacks online. Tap into this propensity – don't forget, the show alongside the tell it makes explanation explicit and intentional, and it builds learner autonomy. It also saves time and allows learners the opportunity to understand and get on with the work more swiftly – clockwork!

The same is true of anything you can pass around for learners to handle. That could be coins, stamps, medals, badges, fabric samples, instruments, navigational equipment, tools, spices, pottery, plants, apparatus – any sort of relic or artefact that can be passed around adds another dimension to the lesson. The fact that learners have had a moment to examine the object makes it personal. Object loan boxes from subject-linked organisations can really bring lessons to life. A memorable Year 9 lesson that we ran involved World War One related artefacts borrowed from Cumbria's Museum of Military Life. Our intention was to secure knowledge and lay the foundation for some later GCSE work on medicine through time. The prosthetic thumb we passed around is still a talking point several years later!

3. Find and fix

'Find and fix' is a great technique to empower your learners. Simply put, you present them with a piece of work and get them to find any errors and fix them. This can be used in multiple ways, such as checking starting points, for revision, as a form of peer assessment, to check understanding – there are so many permutations.

One practical way to do this that has wide appeal in classroom practice is to pretend an uber-credible colleague has had a go at something, which is then riddled with mistakes: units missing, incorrect labels, pedestrian vocabulary, incorrect calculations, incorrect tenses, structural errors, questionable reasoning – whatever it might be relative to your subject. Present this piece of work to the learners and ask them to review it carefully to 'find and fix' the errors. These can be quantified up front, or for added challenge, set up an error hunt without guidance. This unpicking and correcting builds confidence, competence, oracy skills and class camaraderie – a precursor to and sustainer of a clockwork classroom.

Say, for instance, there are nine errors in the piece of work, and you have 16 pairs of learners working on the same document. Set a whole-class target in terms of how many errors will be found collectively. The total here if everyone found everything would be 144. Ask the class to predict how many might be found collectively. For example, let's say on average they find six errors per pair, which would total 96 errors found as a class. You can garner learner buy-in by encouraging them to think about how many errors they could find, setting themselves a composite target and then move this on to how many they could challenge themselves to fix, striving towards high-quality outcomes based on collective strength. Magma Maths keeps a running record digitally, visibly and automatically. I have seen how motivational this is in classrooms in Glasgow. This idea of collective strength is a powerful one, and it's a recurring theme in school and this book. Harness peer power for the greater good whenever you can. The idea and Jürgen Klopp's 'obsession with collective identity' are explored further in *Fortitude* (Daisley, 2023).

A fabulous 'find and fix' example I saw was at Rainford High School whereby the principal, Mr Young (a historian), had (apparently) tried to answer six maths questions based on fractions, decimals and percentages. Year 7 marked his 'attempt', and many found that Mr Young had got two correct but four incorrect. They had to find the wrong answers and fix them, writing kind, specific and helpful feedback. The mistakes were based upon common errors made by learners of that age and stage. The kinds of advice were so insightful: 'I can see what you did here sir...' 'Don't worry Mr Young, it was an easy mistake to make...' 'Here's a way to remember this so you will be less likely to do it again...' 'Maybe you should come to the lunchtime help club?' The feedback was such high quality, since it was being given to the principal, and the activity had been carefully crafted with high expectations in mind to seek proof of understanding. The learner success rate in terms of identifying and correcting errors was high. This ties in with Barak Rosenshine's principles of instruction. His research advocates an optimal success rate of 80% – a benchmark that balances challenge and attainability (Clark, 2025a).

Mr Richardson in the maths department at Portobello High School, Edinburgh likes 'find and fix' activities because he feels they help learners to fully communicate mathematical thought. They require clarity and deep understanding.

This **composite approach** can be applied to all sorts of tasks and situations, and creates classroom connoisseurs to reinforce that important sense of belonging, collegiality and community. It increases participation ratios and teambuilding too, due to the accountability that being part of the whole class entails.

4. Peer marking agreement

In the previous section, the learners gave guidance in a formal and respectful way. They were corresponding with Mr Young, the headteacher. This type of exchange might be a useful precursor to learners liaising with each other, setting the standard and reinforcing high expectations. Either way, a peer marking agreement that all learners sign up to certainly cements classroom accountability. It ensures up-front clarity about the rules of engagement. It is almost like a charter or an official public document, outlining the expectations that can act as a preventative strategy, so thereafter there is no debate about what is required. Have it displayed on the wall or in books for ongoing reference with the signatories clear.

It is best to co-create a peer marking agreement so it being done *by* and *with* learners, rather than *to* learners. This way learners take some ownership and are more likely to be invested in the process; it has value for them. Ask learners what good feedback should look like. Clearly there will be task-specific features, but try to keep the agreement general in terms of being kind, specific and helpful – essentially does it pass the 'move me on' test? Are the next steps to success provided? If not, clearer, more prescriptive guidance is needed.

An example might go as follows, and you could steer the class towards something along these lines if needs be – you are the final arbiter.

- Have I been **kind** and identified something to commend and continue?

- Have I **specifically** picked out something that can be improved?

- Have I been **helpful** and suggested precisely *how* the work can be improved?

5. Frame it and tame it

Marking can be the bane of teachers' lives, taking up inordinate amounts of time. Teachers are often on the lookout for shortcuts or systems that can remain impactful while involving less clockwatching. 'Four quarters marking' (as recommended by Dylan Wiliam) has gained traction (Clark, 2025a) as a time-saving approach to incorporate detailed marking, skimming, and peer and self-assessment.

Something I have noticed when working with learners and teachers in schools on peer feedback is that often learners would prefer it if other learners (and even teachers for that matter) didn't directly write on their work. It can be seen as spoiling the initial effort to some extent. When I have spoken to learners about this, while some don't mind, some have confirmed they would prefer it if it could be avoided.

A mechanism to prevent this is to use an overlay – a transparent frame for the peer marker to write on. These can be made by using A3 laminating pouches. First, I get A3 card (brightly coloured can be appealing) and cut an A4 aperture out of each piece. To save time, mark on the A4 aperture, stack up about six pieces at once, lean on them and cut using a Stanley knife. Then I put each frame into a pouch, laminate and voilà!

Frames should be handy for learners to use, on a helpdesk or shelf, for instance, so they can automatically 'level up' each other's work by framing it and taming it. This prevents wait time in class and leads to less dependence on the teacher and greater self-regulation. If the class is already equipped with a peer marking agreement and learners know how to go about being kind, specific and helpful – better still! They will hopefully know what excellence looks like. Standards have been set, and they may even have a WAGOLL to refer to by way of a worked example, depending on the differing levels of scaffolding needed. It is best to start with something straightforward and quantifiable – factual recall, for instance – to set the ball rolling before moving on to more forensic feedback approaches. The receiver of the feedback can then remove the overlay and action the suggested corrections, closing the gaps as necessary to improve their work based on peer guidance. The frames can be cleaned and re-used repeatedly.

An interesting phenomenon I have noticed is that learners seem keener to close gaps identified by their peers than those identified by their teachers. For instance, I was filming a lesson and one 14-year-old learner said to their partner, 'I would probably give you 9/10.' Incredulous, the recipient of the score protested and said, 'Why isn't it worth 10/10?' The teacher noted that if *he* had issued a score of 9/10, the learner would have thought, 'Happy days, 90%, I'll take that, I'm off for lunch!' Certainly, the young person would not be as concerned about the missing mark, the rationale or a desire to close the gap.

There was an obvious increased impetus to find the missing mark when it had been withheld by a classmate. This might be to do with the need for respect and the desire to look competent in front of others (usually peers) whose opinions sometimes matter more to learners. This leads to motivation. It's all part of creating a climate of high expectations with high challenge and high trust as part of a supportive environment. If we can find opportunities to promote this, we are perhaps helping to minimise 'belonging uncertainty' and creating a shared experience 'so learners feel it is okay to have a go; encouraging learners to attribute their success or failure to things they can change' (Coe et al., 2020).

In this instance, the two teenagers then debated in detail the marking rubric and reached consensus that 9/10 was in fact fair, but how to make it 10 had been thoroughly explored. Connoisseurs were being created.

Clearly, judicious use of learner pairings is needed here. This comes from having up-to-date intel on your learners in terms of who will work best with who, to genuinely enter into the debate with a view to making bona fide steps forwards. The role of the teacher as a detective is ongoing.

At Haydock High School in Merseyside in the maths department, each frame has a hole punched in the corner, and they hang from individual learner desks attached by treasury tags to hooks, so they are immediately available for learners as and when required. Once learners have completed their work, they are self-sufficient to help each other improve. It is said to have been a game changer, with less wait time and more learner autonomy – clockwork!

6. Ready for a receipt?

Any commodity of value tends to have a receipt attached. This is proof of a significant transaction. Learners understand the value represented by a receipt from their daily lives. This same principle can be applied when learners submit important work. Ask the learner: 'Are you ready for a receipt?' In other words, are they ready to complete the transaction? Is what they have done of the highest value, completed to the best of their ability?

The hope is that the learners will of course be connoisseurs by now (once you have exposed them to these strategies and underpinning principles!) and so they won't submit anything second-rate, because it wouldn't be valuable or precious enough. In my experience, learners invariably have asked for more time to refine their work before submission, thus leading to an improved outcome. I tended to get a receipt pad with carbon copy paper. On this I would write the date and the key enquiry question learners were submitting, then sign it and ceremoniously hand them the receipt – deal sealed!

7. Genius bank

A genius bank is a place that learners can go to at lunch or break to get help from others. The others can be at any age and stage, and the genius bank can have different offerings on different days. I have seen this idea successfully in action at St Thomas Aquinas School in Glasgow, where the iGenius bank is a place to get iPad help. The school has a central desk in the social areas, which is manned by learner experts from across the school (in this case digital ambassadors – the school is an Apple Distinguished School) who give their time to help others.

This could of course have a corresponding online equivalent as breaktimes are often too short. However, there is something quite magical about the exchanges I have witnessed between learners in genius banks.

I saw something similar at Accrington Academy when Nathan Ashman was lead teacher for new technologies. In that case, the desk was branded with graphics, on castor wheels and could easily be set up in different parts of the school. Younger learners can help older ones, or teachers (digital dinosaurs like me!) could get tech help too. It is apparent that stage, not age, is the defining factor in technical connoisseurship.

8. Work selfies

Learners will hopefully increasingly know when they have hit the sweet spot and their work is progressing. For instance, when learners are proud of something they have achieved in the D&T department at Pendle Vale College in Nelson, Lancashire, they can indicate that they would like a 'work selfie'. This involves (when it's a tangible creation or book work) taking a clothes peg from a board and attaching it to their work to indicate to the teacher that they would like a picture sent home. This can be via text or QR code or whatever mechanism your school uses. To ensure this is a special occasion and prevent this being onerous admin, there are limits set as to how many times this can happen. Three times a year is typically a good threshold, giving your learners an opportunity to celebrate when a technique has been mastered or a project completed. Learners are aiming high and the audience effect is activated.

9. Super scholars

Use of language can reinforce excellence and self-belief, propelling learners forwards, making an individual quest a shared one: 'Nothing sustains motivation better than belonging to the tribe' (Clear, 2018). In a classroom setting, referring to learners as chemists, musicians, linguists, creators, engineers or readers, for instance, can have the same satisfying effect. When individuals identify with something, they are more likely to commit to daily routines and habits that will help further their self-belief and embed that identity, helping behaviours to last in the long run.

10. Learning detectives

As learners become more proficient, deepen understanding and master skills, they may be able to detect the extent of learning and understanding in others. If this is the case, perhaps activate 'learning detectives'. This means that learners have a 'licence' or warrant to question others, as outlined in 'experts in the room' in chapter three, section three.

Connoisseurship is something to be aspired to and prized. We are hopefully encouraging 'the ability to recognise deep patterns beneath surface differences ... domain-specific knowledge with boundary-crossing competencies' (Kirschner, Hendrick and Heal, 2025).

Takeaways – aim to create classroom connoisseurs

- Unpick, list and try to replicate quality features in your discipline.
- Seek out opportunities to **show** as well as tell.

- Finding and fixing mistakes is a great way for learners to show understanding and demonstrate proficiency.

- To ensure clarity of expectations, ask all to sign up to a peer marking agreement.

- 'Frame it and tame it' is a great mechanism for opening up peer marking discussions.

- Consider issuing receipts for highly prized work.

- Set up a bank of learners who staff a helpdesk or similar to assist others.

- Provide learners with the opportunity to have a photo of quality work sent home or to a loved one.

- Use specialised language to band learners together as being skilled in their endeavours.

- Activate learners to detect and discuss learning with others.

Now it's your turn

- Use the template on page 102 to have a go at some of the 10 strategies that underpin the principle of 'creating classroom connoisseurs'.

- Remember to persevere in order to make approaches routine.

- Set yourself one or more intentions and pledge to review your ongoing progress.

Recommended reading

- *Berger's An Ethic of Excellence in Action* – Sonia Thompson.

- *Outstanding Teaching: Teaching Backwards* – Andy Griffith and Mark Burns.

Chapter 6 map
Classroom commandos

1		Role models – pay it forward
2		Using analogies
3		Thunks and Fermi questions
4		Teach by numbers
5		Prevent clocking off by avoiding white noise
6		Cognitive load theory and cognitive offloading

Chapter 6:
Classroom commandos

'When the going gets tough, the tough get going.' Frank Leahy

A commando is a combatant, a member of an elite special operations force. Commandos are selected based upon having high levels of mental and physical resilience, teamwork and problem-solving skills, calculated risk-taking capabilities, willingness to learn, bravery, willpower, a sense of responsibility, flexibility, secrecy and adaptation. While this clearly doesn't wholly apply to a classroom situation, there are aspects of commando characteristics that would certainly be useful for both teachers and learners to have or aspire to in helping lessons to run smoothly. Namely, once learners have bought in, they need skills that keep them on track.

I am reminded of my brilliant NQT mentor Jean Wirth, who said in 1993 that teaching was 'like a military campaign' with the teacher needing to anticipate, strategise and be 'at least one step ahead of the learners', having conducted a thorough pre-mortem. There was clarity around a shared mission, however that might work in your subject (e.g. a route map or a topic overview). In history, the direction of travel is indicated by an enquiry question that arouses curiosity with a puzzle to solve. I don't want anyone to feel like they're going into battle against adversaries, and this is not what Jean meant. Her point always was that we (teacher and learner) were on the **same side**. There was clarity around a shared mission. Jean encouraged us to create a culture where learners knew you cared and would never give up on them. We communicated an expectation of success using phrases like:

- 'I know you can do this.'
- 'Impressive problem-solving skills there.'
- 'Everyone is having their say, you'll crack it!'

This enabled learners to keep going and overcome obstacles. Through building relationships deliberately, caring about learners and their cultures, and consequently referring to, acting upon and using learned information, we were becoming 'warm demanders' (Bondy and Ross, 2008). Jean never used this phrase, but aspects of this approach certainly applied. The 'warm' aspect involves building intentional relationships, and the 'demanding' aspect relates to expecting great things and convincing learners of their brilliance (Cabeen, 2024).

Similarly, the hope was that learners wouldn't want to disappoint or give up on us teachers either. It was a two-way street, and we were advancing together. If teachers have this outlook, the dispositions of the learners become the focus. Learners build their abilities to maintain momentum, be forward-facing, be their own teachers and keep the end goal in their sights. At the same time, the teacher is leading and intelligence gathering, activating, challenging and processing praise, while acknowledging self-regulation, determination and independence.

A 'mention in dispatches' is formal recognition of meritorious activity in the military. The educational equivalent – a postcard or phone call home – can work wonders in terms of keeping learners committed to the cause. I have seen immediate, tangible token gathering at Yewdale Primary, Carlisle and St Thomas Aquinas, Glasgow, as well as the awarding of kudos via digital badges on online platforms.

Commandos are famed for their tough ethos. In school contexts much is written about the 'R' word, resilience – having grit and a growth mindset. All valid admirable qualities that will help learners to 'slay' when it comes to ticking off and finalising what needs to be done (my girls tell me 'slay' is a shortcut word that will help avoid cognitive overload, and if you work in education, you'll know what it means!).

What constitutes and controls inner strength is complex. In his book *Fortitude,* Bruce Daisley (2023) writes of 'the myth of resilience and the secrets of inner strength'. He sees the twin pillars of identity and control as being key to personal fortitude, but they have a group aspect to them too. 'The group works everywhere' and so we are missing a trick if we don't harness the power of the group (i.e. the learners in the classroom) to help develop fortitude (for more on this, see chapter four).

Most of us will have to draw upon our inner strength at some point in our lives. Some earlier than others, and some more regularly than others. Sometimes we need to dig deep to triumph. Sometimes it is simply to get by, or we may face adversity through a very difficult set of circumstances. This doesn't necessarily happen more as we grow older. We must avoid making assumptions. Some of our learners will have faced, overcome and be dealing with bigger obstacles than some adults can possibly imagine. How well we navigate the various situations we find ourselves in seems to be partially linked with how we are wired, and so much of the human brain is yet unknown. However, having dependable others (a teacher can often take this role) as a support mechanism is invaluable. Encouraging learners to feel a sense of belonging and be ambitious for those in the class can lead to a critical mass of learners ready to support each other.

I have taught 'medicine through time' for many years. I can't help but think about how much is still unknown, despite the phenomenal advances in medicine. In particular, much about how our minds and thought processes work is still a mystery. So aside from these much bigger questions, far beyond the remit of this book, how do we encourage learners to become 'classroom commandos'?

1. Role models – pay it forward

Having role models is a perennial part of growing up. Most young people have heroes or those they are inspired by. In my day in the 1980s, this took the form of pop stars and posters on the bedroom wall: Duran Duran, Spandau Ballet, U2! Who were yours?

In recent times with developments in technology this has become more dynamic. The worrying rise of influencers in some quarters has taken a distinctly sinister turn. Patrick Roach – general secretary of the National Association of Schoolmasters Union of Women Teachers (NASUWT) – highlighted the alarming rise in misogyny and other negative behaviours linked to social media and certain online influencers at his final conference address in April 2025. There are no easy answers to this. A multifaceted approach including stricter regulation of social media is needed to counter the insidious effects of the rapidly evolving online world.

Government-backed plans for schools in England unveiled in December 2025 involve teachers being given training to identify and tackle misogyny in the classroom, while high-risk learners could be sent on behavioural courses as part of a strategy to halve violence against women and girls (VAWG) in the next decade. Prime Minister Keir Starmer encouraged a 'positive, aspirational vision for boys and men' (Kotecha and Shearing, 2025).

One classroom-based way to make role models proximal and relatable is to use inspirational individuals from *within* the school and community. It is possible to achieve this by enlisting the help of older current learners and former learners to pay their wisdom forward to those less experienced. For instance, ask examination class members (GCSE, Scottish Highers) to speak to non-certificated classes. Similarly, ask A-level students to speak to GCSE groups. Depending on the nature of the individuals concerned and school set up, this can be done within lessons, at assembly and at parents'/information/awards evenings.

Professor Stuart Kime, at researchED in Edinburgh, 1 November 2025, spoke about older learners writing letters back to 'normalise the struggle' as a way of removing 'belonging uncertainty'. At St Aidan's we sent letters from secondary back to feeder primary schools to reassure, encourage and propel.

Teachers who have always looked to promote inspirational individuals, whether in lessons, assemblies or awards events, may well redouble their efforts. It is now more important than ever to place emphasis on individuals that learners can learn from. Aimed at young adults, *Feminist History for Every Day of the Year* by Kate Mosse (2025) may well prove to be a valuable resource in this regard. Promotion of positive male role models can help detoxify the social media 'manosphere' (Hern, 2024).

Honours or dux (from the Latin *ducere* – 'to lead') boards are a common feature of schools in England and Scotland. This is an opportunity to celebrate success and put the names of the achievers up in lights. We taught a world champion wrestler in Carlisle! I have also seen halls of fame with photographs and achievements at several schools. This needn't be the preserve of the PE department; all manner of success in varied fields should be celebrated.

Looking ahead to careers options, tapping into alumni can serve several purposes. It makes the next step for learners attainable and authentic since someone who used to sit in your actual classroom is called back as living proof of the next level of possibility. It can prevent possible pitfalls too, since it provides information about 'things I wish I'd known' and guidance to those who are now on that same mission.

Taking it further in a content-based subject-specific way as a history department, we inspired our Year 9 learners to see things differently by enlisting the help of senior community members. Our school hall was opened to a local bowls club who arrived with mats and bowls every

Thursday morning. After some conversations, we discovered one lady in her seventies had worked at Bletchley Park codebreaking, and another gentleman in his eighties had formed part of the team manning Arctic convoys. Through them we contacted other veterans' groups and invited several to speak to our young people about their experiences. It was one of the best school experiences I ever had the honour to take part in. Beyond learning about World War Two, the learners had a newfound admiration for these members of the community. One boy said to me, 'Respect to these guys like, eh? You see them sitting on the bus with white hair and just think they're old and we have nothing in common, but they were actually young once and they led wild lives. I won't look at them in the same way again.' Quite remarkable.

We went on to deepen understanding by using artefacts from the collection at Cumbria's Museum of Military Life to exemplify the powerful stories. With help from the maths department and some cross-curricular links we even managed to get our hands temporarily on an Enigma machine. Some of these real local influencers went on to be mentors, and I'm fully convinced the whole experience helped to develop and maintain learners' commando characteristics.

2. Using analogies

Supporting understanding with analogies is a natural process that even young children can grasp. Comparing something relatively unknown with something generally well known reduces processing load. Analogies enable personal meaning-making, so teachers must create a safe classroom environment and address peer dynamics to ensure learners can – as far as possible – openly and honestly contribute and perhaps create their own. This link to learner experience may well encourage commando-type metacognitive thinking and techniques to solve problems and tackle new scenarios by thinking about previous successes. Use of analogies forms a helpful part of most teachers' repertoires. They can be structural, functional or both. Structural analogies draw parallels between appearances, physical organisations or structures: 'the earth is like an orange'. Functional analogies draw parallels between the way things operate: 'the brain is like a computer' or 'the feudal system is like the way the school is structured' (Newton, 2000).

Analogies can also be used as a means of changing perspectives, and I have seen this used to great effect when trying to build resilience in classrooms. For example, the infamous Peter Kay clip comparing 'one-dip' Rich Tea biscuits that fall apart when the going gets tough to Hobnobs – the 'commando' of biscuits – which are robust and ready to 'say' 'dip me again' when the hot beverage arrives (Creber, 2015). This of course presupposes knowledge of the biscuits, which in my experience has always been validated, but other biscuits are available! Of course, it's not necessarily as straightforward as this, but the analogy is certainly memorable, reduces processing load and in my experience, has the desired effect.

The message is certainly made clear by the popular 'stuck on an escalator' clip. In this scenario, an escalator breaks down and the two people on it come to a standstill. They fail to move themselves forwards when the obvious solution is to walk. This clip reveals that there often isn't a need to wait for help and reinforces the importance of agency and action. It exaggerates the neediness of those who are 'stuck' and can encourage conversations around learner 'stuckness' routines.

3. Thunks and Fermi questions

You may be familiar with Thunks. When I first heard of them, I thought, 'No way, they are not for me.' I was closed-minded. I couldn't see how they would work, but therein lies a masterclass in missing the point. Even if I thought they might not suit *my* way of thinking, I was ignorantly and arrogantly debarring the 300-plus learners I taught weekly from this opportunity to unlock their thinking.

A Thunk is 'a beguiling question about everyday things that stops you in your tracks and helps you to start to look at the world in a whole new light' (Gilbert, 2007). Thunks grew out of Gilbert's work helping children to develop a more philosophical way of thinking.

Even though I thought Thunks weren't for me I could see some merit, and so I shared my copy of *The Little Book of Thunks* with Haydock High. One of the drama teachers was working with Year 10s on a tense courtroom scene on capital punishment. She wanted to reveal understanding and generate thinking so she asked the class, 'If capital punishment was a food, car or item of clothing, what would it be?' She knew this was accessible and there was no right or wrong answer.

One boy replied, 'It would be a food, a dish of cold custard as revenge is a dish best served cold.' The drama teacher was astounded. This was a young person who didn't often speak out and using Thunks had unlocked something in him, a type of conversation kindling. The teacher felt self-esteem had been boosted. It was so worthwhile, as he came to life and got further involved. What was notable was how the learners then proceeded to run with the questioning between themselves. There was a 'contagiousness about such thinking' (Gilbert, 2007) in the lesson, and then I caught the bug! Commando-style, we were propelled to keep going.

I transferred the idea to my history classroom and tried, 'If the Treaty of Versailles was a food, colour or animal, what would it be?' I asked the Year 9 class to think for at least 30 seconds – 'don't skimp on the think' (Inner Drive, 2025) – then pair and share for 90 seconds to pick one and justify it. Tyler and Kyle on the back row decided it would be a food that tasted bitter, because the terms of the treaty left a bitter aftertaste in the mouths of the German people. I asked them, 'What makes you say that?' They went on to explain about reparations and the demilitarised zone. Clearly the Thunk had been a 'thinking worthy prompt' (Clark, 2025b) that led to reasoning, explanation and connection, stretched thinking, and developed discussion.

The quirky nature of Thunks makes learners think and enjoy the intellectual challenge. This modelling of inquisitiveness can help create a classroom culture of enquiry. The call of 'it's a bad heid' (meaning 'my head hurts') from learners is a good thing in Carlisle since it means they are thinking deeply to solve a conundrum or puzzle. I have seen skills of hypothesising, evaluating, persuading, thinking quickly and more when learners are agile-minded and thinking flexibly. This lack of friction leads to smooth-running, learner-led lesson segments, and when it takes off and learners are asking most of the questions, it really is magic!

There is such an art to questioning in the classroom, and getting it right isn't easy. I was in awe of the effortless way in which my more expert, experienced and esteemed colleagues managed this when I was a new teacher. Still now, I am always learning. I'd urge you to learn from others in action, or be watched and seek feedback through the 'have a go' template at the end of the book. The more I watched and thought, the more I realised success came from my colleagues being masters of the content and the direction of travel. They were often being brave in terms of how they mixed it up and presented it. Sometimes feigning ignorance and asking hypothetical and counterfactual questions, this blew my mind! Varying the approach is encouraged in Kate Jones's excellent book *A Little Guide for Teachers: Questioning for Teaching and Learning* (Jones, 2025b).

'How many blades of grass on a football pitch?' Another way of encouraging learner questioning and lateral thinking is using Fermi questions like this one. These are 'order of magnitude problems', which feature in Level 3 core maths and some physics specifications. In the real world, they are 'back of an envelope' calculations used by engineers, scientists and businesspeople to approximate a plausible numerical answer when precise data is unavailable.

The classic conundrum is 'How many piano tuners does a city need?' In this case, the problem solver thinks about the population, the number of people likely to have pianos, how frequently the pianos need tuning and consequently the demand, leading to likely numbers of gainfully employed piano tuners.

The questions are named after Italian physicist Enrico Fermi, who won the 1938 Nobel Prize in physics and is renowned for being part of the Manhattan Project and the creator of the world's first nuclear reactor. Useful classroom examples that really get learners thinking and questioning can be found within Stem resources produced by the National STEM Learning Centre based at the University of York, like 'How many dump trucks would it take to move Mount Fuji?' and 'How to run a top-notch burger bar?' (University of York, n.d.). Of course, learners can go on to devise their own Fermi questions. The transfer of movement from teacher to learner is an overriding theme of the book – clockwork!

4. Teach by numbers

When Mr Hurst at St Aidan's County High School, Carlisle began his assemblies, he would start with clear mission objectives and a clarity of orders (like a commando): 'Good morning everybody, I have three things to discuss...' It was quantifiable, impactful and, most importantly, memorable. This power of three in public speaking is nothing new: the tricolon rhetoric device has been used for centuries to persuade, influence and even manipulate. Famous triplets are everywhere and for all ages. You know them:

- 'I came, I saw, I conquered.'
- 'Education, education, education' – Tony Blair's mantra for prioritising schools in his 1997 campaign.
- 'The good, the bad and the ugly.'
- 'See it, say it, sorted.'

It works by tapping into our cognitive preference for the smallest number of elements needed to make a pattern. Three is a number that audiences are naturally inclined to recognise and resonate with.

So how does this relate to the classroom? It offers precision, which is important to learners. If you say to your class 'Have a quick chat' or 'Talk among yourselves', your instruction is vague. Learners' conversations will simply drift. It is better to ask them for three reasons or three examples (or another sensibly chosen number) related to your topic. This provides a focus and gives learners a target to aim for, which makes them much more inclined to get involved and even go beyond what is expected. By aiming higher, learner staying power is encouraged.

Consider setting a time constraint too. Visual timers can be transformatory in helping learners hold themselves and each other to account. If appropriate, encouraging learners to keep an eye on the clock can be good practice for the inevitable time pressure reality of external exams and the world of work. It encourages consensus, and the need to reach decisions and complete tasks. Clearly you can scaffold discretely and accordingly as you range around activating and challenging learners. There are many online variations of a visual timer. Two websites I have seen used to great effect in classrooms are www.classroomscreen.com with all kinds of functionality beyond the timer and www.classtools.net. Give teach by numbers a go, as it's a tiny tweak which can lead to big improvements in outcomes.

5. Prevent clocking off by avoiding white noise

Maintaining impetus is vital to keep learners focused. My classroom experiences have shown there is a real danger of teachers becoming white noise (I'm using the term 'white noise' colloquially here to mean indistinct background sounds). Teachers sometimes have a tendency to overexplain and keep some learners who already understand waiting. Learners go from room to room, teacher to teacher, having the same messages reinforced, usually about learning dispositions (especially in the run-up to exams), and it can lose impact.

Make what you say meaningful. Sometimes less is more. Carefully say what needs to be said, and set learners off. If you hear or find yourself constantly repeating procedural instructions, it is probably time to change tack. Talk quietly to individuals if needs be. Try to develop non-verbal cues so the soundtrack of your lesson lands with the learners, and they can crack on undisturbed… by you! To take a commando angle, think of it as maintaining radio silence to avoid confusion while the mission is underway.

Some teachers I know can't help themselves from interrupting the flow. It often stems from a lack of a pre-mortem. To create a clear demarcation between teacher exposition and learners working, some teachers I know use quiet instrumental music. These may be extreme cases, but we are all guilty to some extent of not letting learners get on. When we were teaching about the medieval times, members of staff along the history corridor were known to have Gregorian chants softly playing in the background. The geographers up the stairs loved it!

6. Cognitive load theory and cognitive offloading

Cognitive load theory (CLT) 'is the single most important thing for teachers to know' (Dylan Wiliam, quoted in Lovell, 2020). CLT is built on a model of the human memory system that suggests that working memory is limited.

Cognitive offloading through physical actions like writing information down or typing it into a notes app on a mobile phone can help overcome the well-established capacity limits of working memory (Jones, 2025a). This is instinctive, and techniques vary depending on the situation.

Commandos are not the only profession that require keeping their working memories primed. I remember as a child my mam would have sticky notes everywhere in the kitchen with shopping lists, phone numbers, recipes and TV recommendations to help with her cognitive offloading at home, as professionally she was a busy psychiatric nursing sister in an NHS hospital. A rather different, more high-tech example is my youngest daughter's friend. He has recently started training to be an air-traffic controller. He's in a high-pressure situation with masses of information coming at him, and the need for efficient cognitive offloading is vital. The best ways of making connections and methods of remembering them are constantly developing with technological advances and through the work of cognitive scientists.

We clearly need to plan lessons and design our curriculums to avoid overloading learners' working memories so that learning can take place efficiently. **Intrinsic cognitive load** is the core learning we want learners to be placing emphasis on. **Extraneous cognitive load** is what teachers seek to reduce by an efficiently focused manner and structure of instruction. The fundamental recommendation of CLT is to reduce extraneous load through good instructional design and optimise intrinsic load (this might mean reduce, increase or maintain depending on the situation; it isn't a precise science).

Reducing extraneous load

This is almost always the goal in a busy classroom.

- I'm attempting to cut to the chase here and reduce your extraneous load through bulletproof definitions. This is one of my favourite suggested ways of preventing the redundancy effect – eliminate unnecessary information which might distract from the core material.

- Think of it in terms of **homing in on the key takeaways**. In essence, be clear about where to place emphasis. Keep the primary learning goal in mind and stick to it. This frees up available working memory, which can be allocated to intrinsic load which is optimised through appropriate curriculum sequencing.

- **Offering worked examples** (it isn't cheating, contrary to what some teachers fear) refers to the guided practice that learners do following a teacher's initial exposition. 'The most efficient method of studying examples and solving problems [is] to present a worked example and then immediately follow this example by asking the learner to solve a similar problem' – John Sweller (Lovell, 2020).

- **Avoid reading slides out** because by presenting sources of information simultaneously in written and spoken form, both are vying for the same working memory resources, and therefore interfering with each other.

- Similarly, **to avoid a split attention effect** in visual sources, ensure that pieces of information that must be combined are placed together in space and time (Lovell, 2020).

- **Overcoming transient information** is another key lever in securing a clockwork classroom to keep learners going so they don't feel lost. During discussions, have someone act as the scribe to record the key points. With PowerPoints, consider having a 'remember box' where you keep important pieces of information so learners can refer to them whenever needed without having to hold them in their working memories. Progressively revealing animations can also prevent cognitive overload.

- When using film, demos or experiments, consider the guidance 'segment videos into chunks shorter than six minutes' – the median time for watching, following a study of instructional videos (Lovell, 2020). Find videos that take advantage of the modality effect. This means providing words, numbers and pictures together as a form of reinforcement to take advantage of the dual channel nature of working memory. This is something we have endeavoured to do when creating series for BBC Bitesize (BBC, 2026).

Optimising intrinsic load

Intrinsic load relates to the complexity of a task. This often comes into play when learners are working on something they find difficult, so optimising that can help reduce the load.

- Making 'big picture information' available in advance, such as key words, dates and characters, can help optimise intrinsic load.

- Segmenting tasks into bitesize chunks can also be helpful if a learner is overloaded by complexity and difficulty.

- Templates to help learners 'box it off' by filling in finite spaces are really helpful. It appeals to a desire for completionism and many learners will persist much more readily than if faced with a blank sheet of paper.

From all this and probably our own experience, it is clear our brains were designed for 'having ideas not holding them', as said by Oliver Caviglioli and David Goodwin in their book *Organise Ideas*. This book is a fantastic resource for showcasing how 50 teachers have developed and used tools in their lessons to help learners manage cognitive load.

Using these techniques and taking these actions can support learners' learning and encourage them to keep going. Why not pick a suggestion that applies to your teaching and give it a go?

Learners should also be encouraged to self-manage their cognitive load. It is important that they have the power in their hands to increasingly take charge of their own learning. Beyond note pads, using tools such as show-me boards, iPads and films can enable learners to take control. Another way that I know appeals from classroom experience is creating flashcards using the Anki app, as recommended by Daisy Christodoulou (2020). Packs of cards can be made with questions, then the cards are dealt in a customised way based on gaps in remembering following analysis of how much a learner can recall. These techniques mean that learners are less likely to feel overwhelmed, empowering them to resist the tendency to give up and so keeping going – commando style!

Takeaways – motivate, activate and challenge

- Think carefully about use of role models and, if possible, use those linked to school.
- Analogies are brilliant aids in teaching for understanding.
- Consider using Thunks and/or Fermi questions.
- Be precise with numbering and timings.
- Enjoy the silence! Say what you need to say to the whole group succinctly then help smaller groups as needed.
- Take steps to prevent unnecessary cognitive load and provide opportunities for cognitive offloading.

Now it's your turn

- Use the template on page 102 to have a go at some of the six strategies that underpin the principle of 'classroom commandos'.
- Remember to persevere in order to make it routine.
- Set yourself one or more intentions and pledge to review your ongoing progress.

Recommended reading

- *Feminist History for Every Day of the Year* – Kate Mosse.
- *Teaching for Understanding* – Douglas P. Newton.
- *The Little Book of Thunks* – Ian Gilbert.
- *A Little Guide for Teachers: Questioning for Teaching and Learning* – Kate Jones.
- *Sweller's Cognitive Load Theory in Action* – Oliver Lovell.
- *Organise Ideas* – Oliver Caviglioli and David Goodwin.

Have a go!

Date: _____   Class: _____   Time: _____

Weather: ☀ □ ⛅ □

☁ □ ☂ □

Strategy tried: _____

Rationale/underlying principle
Reflections
Next steps – actions
Next steps taken?
Date:

Have a go!

Date: 17th Sept 2026   Class: _Year 7 mixed_   Time: _P3 11.15am_

Weather: ☀-☐ ⛅-☑

☁☐ ☂☐

Strategy tried: _3.1 Issuing jobs_

Rationale/underlying principle

Daring to devolve! I want to encourage self-regulation and autonomy **early** in the school year with first year students so they take responsibility and are less 'needy' and reliant on me. This will help them mix and get to know each other too, I hope.

Reflections

Learners loved the lanyards I had made: resource managers x3, lighting technicians x2 (lights and blinds) and did their jobs well — seemed proud to be asked. Saw some new interactions which was a lovely social spin-off.

Next steps – actions

I will keep them in these roles for two weeks (Andy, Jacqui, Angela, Bryan & Georgie) then re-issue. I might do this randomly next time after initially choosing these candidates who would set a good example and ensure a flying start. I will be sure to contact home/mention on end of term reports.

Next steps taken?

Pack shuffled and new students in place. Two weeks seems like a good duration. It's becoming a norm. Learners say they like it. I will ask them what other jobs I could devolve.

Date: Oct 1st 2026

Taking stock

Timeframe							
After:	Month	☐	Half-term ☐	Term	☐	Year	☐

I have noticed the learners are...

I am doing more of...

I am doing less of...

Pledge – next steps

Signed _____ Date _____

Bibliography

Adams, R. (2024) 'Record numbers of pupils in England absent for long periods, DfE data shows', *The Guardian*. 21 March [Online]. Available at: www.theguardian.com/education/2024/mar/21/record-numbers-of-pupil-absences-in-england-dfe-figures-show (Accessed: 16 February 2026).

Amass, H. (2024) 'Why research must reconnect to the classroom', *TES Magazine*, 21 Feb.

Ball, R. and Fairlamb, A. (2025) *The Scaffolding Effect: Supporting All Students to Succeed*. Abingdon, Oxon: Routledge.

BBC (2026) *Peaceful protests in the 1960s*. Available at: www.bbc.co.uk/bitesize/guides/z2r66g8/video (Accessed: 27 February 2026).

Beard, M. (2015) *Laughter in Ancient Rome: On Joking, Tickling, and Cracking Up*. Oakland, CA: University of California Press.

Beck, I. L., McKeown, M. G. and Kucan, L. (2013) *Bringing Words to Life: Robust Vocabulary Instruction*, 2nd edn. New York, NY: Guildford Press.

Bennett, T. (2020) *Running the Room*. Woodbridge: John Catt.

Berger, R. (2003) *An Ethic of Excellence Grade 3–8: Building a Culture of Craftsmanship with Students*. Portsmouth, NH: Heinemann.

Bishop, C. (2024) 'Swim England's toxic culture must go – it is time for sport to prioritise joy', *The Guardian*. 14 March [Online]. Available at: www.theguardian.com/sport/blog/2024/mar/14/swim-englands-toxic-culture-must-go-it-is-time-for-sport-to-prioritise-joy (Accessed: 1 April 2026).

Bondy, E. and Ross, D. D. (2008) *The teacher as warm demander*. Available at: https://ascd.org/el/articles/the-teacher-as-warm-demander (Accessed: 26 February 2026).

Bones, C., Smith, S. and Longair, S. (2025) 'Reteach History – Sasha Smith and Sarah Longair on the British Empire and its objects', *Reteach History* [Podcast], 25 April. Available at: www.ivoox.com/en/reteach-history-sasha-smith-and-sarah-longair-audios-mp3_rf_145693741_1.html (Accessed: 25 February 2026).

Booth, S. (2024a) 'Almost as many teachers left the profession as entered it last year', *Schools Week*. 6 June [Online]. Available at: https://schoolsweek.co.uk/teaching-workforce-grows-by-just-259-as-recruitment-stalls/ (Accessed: 16 February 2026).

Booth, R. (2024b) '"Happiness recession": UK 15-year-olds at bottom of European satisfaction league', *The Guardian*. 29 August [Online]. Available at: www.theguardian.com/society/article/2024/aug/29/uk-teenagers-low-life-satisfaction-europe (Accessed: 20 February 2026).

Cabeen, J. (2024) *A warm demander approach to school leadership*. Available at: www.edutopia.org/article/warm-demander-approach-administration (Accessed: 16 February 2026).

Camilleri, T., Rockey, S. and Dunbar, R. (2024) *The Social Brain: The Psychology of Successful Groups*. UK: Penguin.

Caviglioli, O. and Goodwin, D. (2021) *Organise Ideas: Thinking by Hand, Extending the Mind*. Woodbridge: John Catt.

Christodoulou, D. (2020) *Teachers vs Tech?: The Case for an Ed Tech Revolution*. Oxford: OUP.

Clark, J. (2024) *Teaching One-Pagers: Evidence-Informed Summaries for Busy Educational Professionals*. Woodbridge: John Catt.

Clark, J. (2025a) *Teaching One-Pagers 2: Evidence-Informed Summaries for Busy Educational Professionals*. London: Hachette Learning.

Clark, J. (2025b) *Think-Pair-Share*. Available at: https://newsletter.jamieleeclark.com/p/think-pair-share (Accessed: 1 April 2026).

Clear, J. (2018) *Atomic Habits*. London: Random House Business.

Coe, R. (2024) *Why you need feedback more than you think you do*. Great Teaching Toolkit, researchED National Conference, London.

Coe, R., Rauch, C. J., Kime, S. and Singleton, D. (2020) *Great teaching toolkit evidence review*. Available at: www.teachertoolkit.co.uk/wp-content/uploads/2020/06/Great-Teaching-Toolkit.pdf (Accessed: 26 February 2026).

Counsell, C. (2024) 'A curriculum should leave pupils bursting to talk – having something to say, a burning desire to communicate it, confident oral expression, wide vocabulary, skill in argument and a will to listen.' *X* (formerly Twitter), 15 March. Available at: https://x.com/Counsell_C/status/1768593140271776033 (Accessed: 19 February 2026).

Counsell, C. (2025) *Christine Counsell NI curriculum – speech on 7 May 2025*. Available at: www.education-ni.gov.uk/publications/christine-counsell-ni-curriculum-speech-7-may-2025 (Accessed: 25 February 2026).

Creber, P. (2015) *Butterfly #15: Setting and selling the vision*. Available at: https://westfieldacademytandl.wordpress.com/2015/01/07/butterfly-15-setting-and-selling-the-vision/ (Accessed: 25 February 2026).

Crome, S. (2023) *The Power of Teams: How to Create and Lead Thriving School Teams*. Woodbridge: John Catt.

Daisley, B. (2023) *Fortitude: The Myth of Resilience and the Secrets of Inner Strength*. London: Penguin.

DfE (2025) *The link between attendance and attainment in an assessment year*. Available at: www.gov.uk/government/publications/link-between-attendance-and-attainment (Accessed: 31 October 2025).

DfE (2026) *Every child achieving and thriving*. Available at: www.gov.uk/government/publications/every-child-achieving-and-thriving (Accessed: 3 March 2026).

Dix, P. (2017) *When the Adults Change, Everything Changes: Seismic Shifts in School Behaviour*. Carmarthen: Crown House.

Eastwood, O. (2022) *Belonging: The Ancient Code of Togetherness*. London: Quercus.

EEF (2021) *Teacher feedback to improve pupil learning*. Available at: https://educationendowmentfoundation.org.uk/education-evidence/guidance-reports/feedback (Accessed: 15 August 2024).

EEF (2025) *Metacognition and self-regulated learning: Guidance report*. Available at: https://educationendowmentfoundation.org.uk/education-evidence/guidance-reports/metacognition (Accessed: 24 February 2026).

Enser, M. (2025) 'Make time for learning', *Teaching It Real*, 5 November. Available at: https://enserm.substack.com/p/make-time-for-learning?utm_source=share&utm_medium=android&r=1nguam&triedRedirect=true (Accessed: 6 November 2025).

Enser, Z. and Enser, M. (2020) *Fiorella & Mayer's Generative Learning in Action*. Woodbridge: John Catt.

Fletcher-Wood, H. (2021) *Habits of Success: Getting Every Student Learning*. Abingdon, Oxon: Routledge.

Francis, B. (2025) *Curriculum assessment and review: Building a world-class curriculum for all: Final report*. Available at: https://assets.publishing.service.gov.uk/media/690b96bbc22e4ed8b051854d/Curriculum_and_Assessment_Review_final_report_-_Building_a_world-class_curriculum_for_all.pdf (Accessed: 19 February 2026)

Gamote, S. and Hyman, P. (2025) *Inside the mind of a 16-year-old*. Available at: https://demos.co.uk/research/inside-the-mind-of-a-16-year-old-from-andrew-tate-to-bonnie-blue-to-nigel-farage-what-do-first-time-voters-think-about-social-media-politics-the-state-of-britain-and-their-futures/ (Accessed: 11 November 2025).

Gibbs, S. and Bean, A. (2025) 'Is didagogy the key to better CPD for teachers?' *TES Magazine*, 22 October.

Gilbert, I. (2007) *The Little Book of Thunks*. Carmarthen: Crown House.

Gilbert, I. (2025) *Essential Motivation in the Classroom: Seven Keys for Unlocking Your Students' Learning*, 3rd edn. Abingdon, Oxon: Routledge.

Gino, F. (2019) *Cracking the code of sustained collaboration*. Available at: https://hbr.org/2019/11/cracking-the-code-of-sustained-collaboration (Accessed: 19 February 2026).

Gov.uk (2024) Pupil absence in schools in England. Available at: https://explore-education-statistics.service.gov.uk/find-statistics/pupil-absence-in-schools-in-england/2023-24-autumn-term (Accessed: 16 February 2026).

Griffith, A. and Burns, M. (2014) *Outstanding Teaching: Teaching Backwards*. Carmarthen: Crown House.

Harvard, B. (2025) *Do I Have Your Attention?: Understanding Memory Constraints and Maximizing Learning*. London: Routledge.

Hattie, J. and Yates, G. (2013) *Visible Learning and the Science of How We Learn*. London: Routledge.

Hern, A. (2024) 'How positive male role models are detoxifying the social media "manosphere"', *The Guardian*. 2 March [Online]. Available at: www.theguardian.com/media/2024/mar/02/positive-male-role-models-detoxifying-social-media-manosphere (Accessed: 27 February 2026).

Historical Association's Secondary Committee (2025) *Driving your discussion*. Available at: www.history.org.uk/secondary/categories/466/resource/11229/driving-your-discussion (Accessed: 17 October 2025).

Hunt, H. (2025) *Wiegman reflects on 'crazy' Euro 2025*. Available at: www.englandfootball.com/articles/2025/Jul/28/sarina-wiegman-euro-2025-reflection-interview-20252807 (Accessed: 29 July 2025).

InnerDrive (2025) *Most teachers skimp on the think in think-pair-share | with Dylan Wiliam*. YouTube video, 14 May. https://youtu.be/mMnAMx9er3o?si=vpoC1OU4axG0rsox (Accessed: 27 February 2026).

Ishak, M., Oderinde, I. and Ahmad, S. (2025) 'The role of metacognitive strategies in enhancing learning outcomes and educational efficiency: A systematic review of quantitative, qualitative and mixed-method studies.' *International Journal of Academic Research in Business and Social Sciences*, 15(4): pp. 81–101.

Jones, K. (2018) *Love to Teach: Research and Resources for Every Classroom*. Woodbridge: John Catt.

Jones, K. (2023) *The curse of knowledge: A cognitive bias all teachers should be aware of*. Available at: https://evidencebased.education/resource/the-curse-of-knowledge-a-cognitive-bias-all-teachers-should-be-aware-of/ (Accessed: 25 February 2026).

Jones, K. (2024) *Feedback: Strategies to Support Teacher Workload and Improve Pupil Progress*. Woodbridge: John Catt from Hodder Education.

Jones, K. (2025a) *Cognitive offloading: what is it and why is it important?* Available at: https://evidencebased.education/resource/cognitive-offloading-what-is-it-and-why-is-it-important-2/ (Accessed: 27 February 2025).

Jones, K. (2025b) *A Little Guide for Teachers: Questioning for teaching and learning*. London: Corwin.

Kara, B. (2025) *Nuthall's Hidden Lives of Learners in Action*. London: Hachette Learning.

Keates, D., Stanford, M. and Goullée, C. (eds.) (2025) *A Practical Guide to Teaching History in the Secondary School*, 2nd edn. Abingdon, Oxon: Routledge.

Kirschner, P. A., Hendrick, C. and Heal, J. (2025) *Instructional Illusions*. London: Hachette Learning.

Kotecha, S. and Shearing, H. (2025) *Boys to be sent on courses to tackle misogyny in schools*. Available at: www.bbc.co.uk/news/articles/c9qednjzwv1o (Accessed: 27 February 2026).

Lovell, O. (2020) *Sweller's Cognitive Load Theory in Action*. Woodbridge: John Catt.

Mackesy, C. (2025) *Always Remember*. London: Penguin Books.

Mannion, J. (2025) *Making Change Stick: A Practical Guide to Implementing School Improvement*. London: John Catt from Hachette Learning.

Masuno, S. (2022) *Don't Worry: 48 Lessons on Achieving Calm*. UK: Penguin.

McLeod, S. (2024) *Expository teaching: Ausubel theory of learning*. Available at: www.simplypsychology.org/expository-method-of-teaching.html (Accessed: 17 August 2024).

Miller, G. A. (1956) 'The magical number seven, plus or minus two: Some limits on our capacity for processing information.' *Psychological Review*, 63(2): pp. 81–97.

Morton, E. (2015) *Battles, Batman and Liberace: A cultural history of capes*. Available at: www.atlasobscura.com/articles/battles-batman-and-liberace-a-cultural-history-of-capes (Accessed: 1 September 2024).

Mosse, K. (2025) *Feminist History for Every Day of the Year*. London: Pan Macmillan.

Myatt, M. (2016) 'Refining the curriculum', *Curriculum 101*, 3 September. Available at: https://marymyatt.substack.com/p/refining-the-curriculum (Accessed: 24 February 2026).

Newton, D. P. (2000) *Teaching for Understanding: What It Is and How to Do It*. London: Routledge.

Nottingham, J. (2023) *The Learning Pit*. Available at: https://learningpit.org/learning-pit/ (Accessed: 3 March 2026).

Oracy Cambridge and Voice 21 (2019) *The oracy skills framework and glossary*. Available at: https://oracycambridge.org/wp-content/uploads/2020/06/The-Oracy-Skills-Framework-and-Glossary.pdf (Accessed: 19 February 2026).

Oracy Education Commission (2024) *We need to talk, 2024*. Available at: https://oracyeducationcommission.co.uk/oec-report/ (Accessed: 22 February 2026).

Oxford University Press (2024) *The Oxford language report 2023–24: Building children's vocabulary at home & school*. Available at: https://fdslive.oup.

com/www.oup.com/oxed/wordgap/Oxford_Language_Report_2023-24_ Building_Vocabulary_At_School.pdf?region=uk (Accessed: 19 February 2026).

Pearce, J. and Moore, I. (2024) *Bjork and Bjork's Desirable Difficulties in Action*. Woodbridge: John Catt.

Perera, A. (2024) *The Hawthorne effect*. Available at: www.simplypsycho logy.org/hawthorne-effect.html (Accessed: 30 August 2024).

Rahnev, D. (2025) 'A comprehensive assessment of current methods for measuring metacognition.' *Nature Communications*, 16(1): p. 701.

Ribosa, J., Corcelles-Secuba, M., Morodo, A. and Duran, D. (2023) 'Reducing teachers' resistance to reciprocal peer observation.' *European Journal of Education*, 59(2): e12606.

Ritchhart, R. (2023) *Cultures of Thinking in Action: 10 Mindsets to Transform our Teaching and Students' Learning*. Hoboken, NJ: Jossey-Bass.

Royle, C. (2023) *Second Set of Eyes: How Great Coaches Become Great Champions*. Independently published.

Sealy, C. (2024) *Oracies not oracy*. Available at: https://primarytimery. com/2024/08/25/oracies-not-oracy (Accessed: 22 February 2026).

Sherrington, T. (2018) 'Great teaching. The power of expectations', *Teacherhead*, 2 September. Available at: https://teacherhead.com/2018/ 09/02/great-teaching-the-power-of-expectations/ (Accessed: 26 October 2025).

Sinfield, K. (2023) *The Extra Mile*. London: Century.

Sotto, E. (2007) *When Teaching Becomes Learning: A Theory and Practice of Teaching*. London: Continuum.

TES (2025) 'Severe student absence increases', *TES Magazine*, 23 October.

University of York. (n.d.) *Fermi problems*. Available at: www.stem.org. uk/resources/library/collection/419670/fermi-problems (Accessed: 27 February 2026)

Wallace, I. and Kirkman, L. (2014) *Talk-Less Teaching: Practice, Participation and Progress*. Carmarthen: Crown House.

Personalised professional development from Hachette Learning Academy

A simple way to boost career progression, staff motivation and educational excellence.

Our online courses are:

 Aligned with **teaching competency frameworks**

 Written by experts in education, including Hachette Learning authors (formerly John Catt)

 Created to enable educators to **develop competencies** linked to their professional development aspirations

 Powered by adaptive learning, to accommodate a diverse range of skills, knowledge and understanding

 Designed to support **effective learning and high-impact teaching**

www.hachettelearning.com/academy